NO ROOM FOR DOUBT

NO ROOM FOR DOUBT

Herbert Lee Williams
Foreword by RAMSEY POLLARD

BROADMAN PRESS
Nashville, Tennessee

© Copyright 1976 ● Broadman Press
All rights reserved
4252-36
ISBN: 0-8054-5236-2

Dewey Decimal Classification: 220.1
Subject Headings: BIBLE—EVIDENCES // AUTHORITY, ETC.
Library of Congress Catalog Card Number: 75-39574
Printed in the United States of America

Dedicated to
THREE WOMEN
*One taught me faith; one
brought me hope; one
gave me love*

and to
THREE MEN
*My soundest investment on
earth, and my surest
reward in heaven*

FOREWORD

This book comes from the heart and pen of a brilliant university professor who writes in such a unique fashion that it will strengthen every believer, and convince many unbelievers who would study its content with open and searching minds. The language is clear, pungent, and illuminating.

Dr. Williams came out of total doubt to a firm, intelligent, and functioning faith in the authenticity of the Bible as God's Word. He properly gives credit to the Holy Spirit working through men in the production of the Bible. His forceful discussion reveals a superb understanding undergirded by scholarly and diligent research. I wish this book might be placed in the hands of every Bible teacher in our seminaries, universities, and colleges.

Dr. Williams is unashamedly Baptist. He teaches a large men's class at Bellevue Baptist Church, Memphis, Tennessee. However, he shows a remarkable spirit of love for those of other faiths. He stresses the free moral agency and responsibility of the individual.

NO ROOM FOR DOUBT is splendid, challenging, and thought-provoking. I sincerely hope it will have a wide circulation. In my humble judgment it is one of the most worthy books I have read.

RAMSEY POLLARD

PREFACE

I was a doubter.

Although I heard the "good news" from an early age, I punctuated it with a question mark rather than an exclamation point. My spiritual feet did not seek out the straight path that leads to the cross, but traveled instead the circuitous route of all disciples of doubt.

The well-worn intellectual hangups that originally tripped a Nicodemus or a Thomas or a Philip—"how can these things be?" . . . "except I see, I will not believe" . . . "show us, and it will suffice us" . . . "and how can we know the way?"—also caused me to stumble.

Like every other doubter I have known, I was quick to defend the honesty and purity of my questioning. I was a seeker after truth. No axes to grind. Perfectly willing to be shown the answers. At least, I thought so.

The suicidal non-answer of atheism was abhorrent to me. For needed identity, the respectable Greek label of "agnostic" seemed to fit comfortably at first. (That is, until some smart-aleck professor pointed out to me its exact Latin cognate: "ignoramus.")

Accurately speaking, I was no agnostic, because I had rather systematically ransacked philosophies and religions and denominational theories in a desperate search for information—until I did master some of the facts. I'm afraid that I was just a plain, colorless doubter.

The most curious fact I acquired eventually was the undeniable worthlessness of the attitude of doubt. The long accumulation of efforts devoted to doubting yielded not a single value that I could point to. It was an honest investment, I kept telling myself. Yet there were no dividends to enrich my personal life or to enhance my worth to those about me. I was past thirty, and the only testimony I had to offer was a quotation from William Lyon Phelps: "My religious faith remains in possession of the field only after prolonged civil war with my naturally skeptical mind." And I wasn't too sure about that.

The light broke in when I made the discovery that my vaunted intellectual integrity was nothing in this world but ordinary, dirt-cheap, human pride. With that out of the way, I was able, for the very first time, to get a good look at the source of all my trouble—and I could hardly believe my eyes. My real problem was ignorance. I mean abysmal, appalling, humiliating ignorance.

You see, what I didn't know was that *doubting is deciding*. I had never caught on to the fact that unbelief is a commit-ment. For some strange reason I had failed to realize that to distrust is to make a dreadful choice. I had been too stupid to perceive that, where God is concerned, so-called mental assent is no assent at all. By clinging to doubt, I was pronouncing God to be a liar and exalting the religion of Satan.

Some simple, nameless man of nearly 2,000 years ago said, "Lord, I believe; help thou mine unbelief." I began to say exactly the same thing. And I got exactly the same results he did. For more than a quarter of a century now, I have made my living in the field of higher education, where relentless inquiry and critical analysis and compara-tive evaluation are the tools with which I work day by day. But, miraculously, I have been able to whistle, while I work, one happy tune without interruption: "Praise God, the doubts are settled, and I know, I know it's real."

Once I got the message loud and clear that in a genuine quest for God's company, "honest doubt" is a delusion, I made an even more staggering discovery. It was about this doubt-demolishing thing called grace. One thing life had taught me to measure properly was the abundance of sin that proliferates all about us. But what a thrill to learn that where sin abounded, grace did much more abound!

Now I know. Every time I come across those words uttered by a first-century doubter, my nervous system floods anew with unspeakable joy and gratitude: "But I obtained mercy, because I did it ignorantly in unbelief." Thanks to this mysterious grace, the religion of Satan is even today losing converts who were once devotees to doubt.

Because I know what it is to live in bondage to doubt and because I have experienced liberating grace, I am under compulsion to relay to you the imperative side of the same first-century message: "Take heed, brethren, lest there be in any of you an evil heart of unbelief, in departing from the living God. But exhort one another daily, while it is called To-day; lest any of you be hardened through the deceitfulness of sin" (Heb. 3:12-13).

That's what doubt is all about. It's the innocent-appearing but arrogant heart-hardener, the captivating deceitfulness of sin. I exhort you today to join me in a departure from doubt. Frankly, there is *no room for doubt!*

HERBERT LEE WILLIAMS

CONTENTS

FOREWORD   vii

PREFACE   ix

INTRODUCTION   13

1. THE FIRST STEP   17
2. A MATTER OF COMMUNICATION   27
3. THE MESSAGE THAT BREATHES   35
4. A HEAVENLY GIFT IN EARTHLY VESSELS   45
5. HOW DID THE BOOKS BECOME **THE BOOK?**   59
6. THE LIBRARY IN YOUR HANDS   77
7. SCIENCE VERSUS SCRIPTURE: NO CONTEST   93
8. LEARNING TO READ   121
9. THE BIBLE—WHO NEEDS IT?   149

INTRODUCTION

This book is based on the simple observation that doubt is an affliction to which all humanity is exposed, as contagious and as widespread as the common cold. Its symptoms are universally the same, with predictable variations from patient to patient. The diagnosis is easy, the remedy is specific, and the cure is infallibly complete and permanent.

Experience with doubt and doubters teaches one thing: despite all appearances, God is not the real target. God is either trusted, or he is feared—but he is not unaffectedly doubted by the sane mind. This is true simply because there is no way to remove the consciousness of God from the human brain. So-called "atheism," in all of its changing political or philosophical or pseudo-scientific forms, is at best a subterfuge, a semantic attempt to get rid of the fear of God.

It is granted that many of the people who are troubled with doubts are under the impression that they are questioning the existence of God. But in actuality their questions are aimed at something else. The conviction upon which this book is formulated is that virtually all doubting can be reduced to three clearly-defined dimensions:

(1) doubts about God's Word (the Bible)
(2) doubts about God's Son (Jesus Christ)
(3) doubts about God's people (the church)

Arguments about God invariably focus on one or all of these points. Ignorance of the Bible, misinterpretation of the redemptive role of Jesus Christ, and confusion about the nature of the church in the world form an equilateral triangle around which doubts endlessly chase themselves.

13

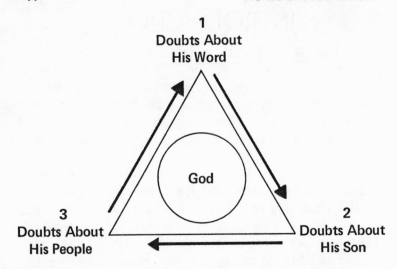

If you aren't convinced that the Bible is the inerrant Word of God, or if you have any uneasy suspicions about its relevance, then naturally you will lack conviction about Christ as the Son of God, because the Bible is the source of all information about Jesus. If you fail to understand and to accept the saviorhood of God incarnate, then his people, who are represented today by the institution he established, will remain a deterrent to you. If you are frightened away by the conflicting claims of denominations and by some of the activities and individuals parading behind them, or if you visualize a "Jesus movement" as something actually independent of the church, you could be expected to develop a distorted appraisal of God's Word, for the church is supposedly where the Bible is taught. Thus, you find yourself turning the same old corner again and again, without ever getting inside this triangle of doubts and drawing closer to the satisfying presence of God.

By resolving legitimate questions concerning the Bible, specific doubts can be erased one by one. Then you'll find that the attitude of doubt has no place left to call home, and will depart of its own accord.

The references to Scripture are all from the King James Version, for no other reason than that it is the version which—despite its age, or perhaps because of it—is to me more expressive and more inspiring than any of the contemporary efforts to improve upon it. In some of the quotations I have taken the liberty of capitalizing all the letters of particular words for emphasis.

Acknowledgements are due not to a few, but to hundreds here and there who have shed gleams of light on my path. "Wherefore, seeing we also are compassed about with so great a cloud of witnesses," humble thanks are expressed to all who have spoken or written one word of truth to me and, thus, shared in the motivation for the preparation of this work.

I am particularly indebted to my pastor, Dr. Adrian Rogers of Bellevue Baptist Church, for his kind permission to quote freely from his Spirit-filled pulpit messages which have inspired millions by radio and television. Special thanks go to Peter E. Gillquist, a former colleague at Memphis State University, for his patient reading and expert critique of the manuscript; and to Dr. Ramsey Pollard, retired pastor and president of the Southern Baptist Convention, for his interest and encouragement in the work.

It has been said that the name of Jesus Christ has set more pens and typewriters in motion than any other influence in world history. I'm glad that mine could be included.

1.
THE FIRST STEP

*The doubter can't find God for the same reason
a thief can't find a policeman.*

So you've got questions. All kinds of questions. Questions about the origin and the destiny of all things, about your place in the universe, about the meaning of life, about moral problems of the day in which you live, about God. That's fortunate, because this book is written for people who have questions—people like you.

Don't abandon your questions. A healthy curiosity is a dead giveaway of a functioning brain and a clear intellect. The inquisitive mind is the one that's likely to come up with the deepest answers. After all, generating questions and collecting answers are as essential to mental development as breathing out and breathing in are to physical well-being.

What is a question but a tool for prying the lid off the unknown? Surely we have a right and an obligation to probe into all the records of the past, into the secrets of the environment about us, and into the possibilities of our future.

In the process, though, we discover something that sobers

us: even the best questions have their limitations. For one thing, they don't always produce answers. More often than not they provide us with only fragments of answers. Sometimes we ask the wrong questions, in which case we get wrong answers.

And there is a point at which the question may become a serious liability instead of a wholesome benefit. That is at whatever point we begin to assume that we are entitled to an answer.

When we begin to demand answers in terms acceptable to us, then we are no longer putting questions to work as useful tools. From that point on, our questions can do us more harm than good, because now we are allowing them to manipulate us. Our formerly creative spirit of inquiry takes on a totally new look as our questions begin to breed in us an attitude of distrust and suspicion toward the object of our curiosity.

What happened? Why do our questions now recoil on us and bring us more frustration than satisfaction? Simply because something from within ourselves has entered the picture—call it self-assumption, self-will, self-pride. We insist on the answers, but we get even fewer than before and those we do get seem to be inadequate and unrewarding. And when we come up with no answer at all, the effect is demoralizing, insulting the ego and dampening the spirit. We are well on the way to becoming a cynical, hardened doubter.

All this is well represented in a little word that the Greeks had for it: *diaporeo*. Literally it means "to be without any resource." Translated into English, it is the familiar *doubt*. That would seem to be the key to the whole problem. When we ask questions, we gamble on the demoralization that may accompany the failure to get answers—unless we are previously fortified by some resource peculiarly qualified to protect against these damaging frustrations.

It becomes obvious, then, that doubting can serve no useful purpose whatever, as it provides nothing we need in the challenging quest for answers. Doubt is a lacking, a void, an absence. It's a negative attitude which cannot accomplish anything in the interest of positive inquiry into problems that are real, pressing, and ever present.

What we must have is a moral resource—something that enables us to live with partial answers or to endure the crush of no answers at all, if that's the situation we find ourselves in. Something that encourages us to go on asking and seeking with the firm expectation of receiving and finding enough to make the whole effort enormously rewarding.

Again, there's a word for it. An English word, this time. And you have already anticipated it: *faith.*

Now, depending on what it is you're really after, you could allow yourself to be turned off right here by a preconceived stereotype of what constitutes faith. This is one of those terms that, just by being pronounced, conjures up a variety of fixed notions, so let's first be sure that we are using the same referents.

Faith, basically, is doing nothing. How's that for a definition? Faith requires no action on our part; it is a completely passive quality. You simply have faith—you don't generate it or create it. Once you have it, faith can grow and develop in strength until it becomes the controlling force in your life. But you can't produce it from within yourself. It comes from an outside source.

Make Up Your Mind

It's like accepting a gift. You have the choice of rejecting the offer of a present, or of accepting it. If you choose to spurn or refuse the gift, that's where you become engaged in active resistance. Now, this resistance to faith is something that you *can* take credit for creating or generating within yourself. For many, this polite refusal escalates into a lifetime of attrition, a war of rebellion against the very suggestion of the existence of faith as a reality.

On the other hand, there is the choice of yielding to this idea in passive surrender and accepting faith as a gift with no strings attached. When we are thus yielded, we are simply acknowledging the presence of a resource that we find otherwise lacking, and we are submitting our total personality to its influence. This is no mere psychological exercise, like some temporary suspension of disbelief, or a realignment of previous concepts in order to establish a fresh point of view. Here is a supernatural resource, something that is beyond the capacity of human thought and yet always available to us.

Selling faith short is one of the easiest things in the world to do, which explains why it is a favorite pastime of skeptics. But faith is by no means a frantic leap in the dark as a desperate, final gesture. Neither is it unthinking submission. It is calculated, willing surrender in which the reasoning powers come into full play.

Faith experiments with the unknown as frankly as do the empirical sciences. But instead of starting with an hypothesis and then searching for data to support or refute that premise, faith is free to start anywhere a need exists, and to press on regardless of what the data—or lack of data—may indicate.

Here's a power, then, that is superior to reason, because reason must work with the materials at hand and can operate only within the framework of its own findings. Faith is unfettered, limitless, beyond the puny restrictions of logic.

But more than that—faith is free for the asking. Not all are gifted with the power of reasoning to any exceptional degree, although some few have reached monumental heights by rigorous training or by natural genius. But the gift of faith is liberally offered to every single one of us, regardless of our state of preparation to receive it.

We don't inherit faith, and we can't acquire it through striving. We can only accept it. But from then on, it is as truly ours as if we had legally fallen heir to it or had come into ownership of it through a lifetime of hard work.

If you mean business about overcoming doubt, you'll have to begin by taking one simple step of faith. Without getting even slightly involved at this point in the endless theological and philosophical debates about infinite issues which are quite beyond the grasp of most of us, let us start at a tangible, identifiable point of departure where you know exactly what you are doing. At least, you will know for sure whether or not you want to take that first step.

And it is a simple move. It is so clear-cut and so obvious that most people consider it something to take for granted, and consequently to ignore, to forget, to avoid being confronted with. Yet it's there, placed in the middle of the river of human history and right across your own stream of consciousness, and it has to be dealt with.

What is it? It is none other than God's Word—a message, a news report, written in bulletins that penetrate, and bound in the visible dimensions of a book. We can't question its existence or pretend it's not important, because the Bible is the most talked-about documentary record in the world.

But we can have many, many doubts about the message this Book contains. What else can you think of offhand that has provoked as many questions, as much criticism, and as long-standing opposition as the Scriptures? Isn't this the first target of the skeptic, this bound volume that lends itself so readily to attack?

> —Isn't it just another book, a part of the literature of antiquity?

> —How can something so fallible as the crafts of copying and printing be expected to preserve the integrity of a message through thousands of years?

> —Who brought the books of the Bible together under one cover, and who gave them such authority anyway?

> —How trustworthy are all these writings gathered from various centuries and localities and languages?

> —Aren't other books just as "inspired" as this one?

> —Don't versions and revisions disagree among themselves? What about the inevitable errors in translation?

> —How relevant can so ancient a message be in our changing times?

Questions like these are germinated by the very fact of

the existence of this mysterious volume. But let's hold them in abeyance for just a little while, with the understanding that we'll get around to all of these questions, and more.

A Place to Begin

Because the Bible challenges you to make an honest decision and an all-out commitment as to whether you will accept it on faith as being what it claims to be—the Word of God—it is the logical place to launch our examination of doubting. Here is a report that asks with mind-reading candor, "Who hath believed our REPORT?" (Isa. 53:1). You are made to feel uneasy by this record that boldly says of itself, "He that believeth not God hath made him a liar; because he believed not the RECORD that God gave of his Son" (1 John 5:10). Assuming unlimited authority, this word demands that you listen to it, on the grounds that "faith cometh by hearing, and hearing by the WORD of God" (Rom. 10:17).

How does one react to such a message? There is only one way. If we are setting out to liquidate doubt, then let's attack it head-on. Even without being sure of what God is like, you have found that it is possible to believe in him. That means you can therefore *believe* God—you can depend on what he *says*. And what does he say? That this is his message, not man's. He affirms that this is his testimony, although it is undeniably packaged in the fragile, vulnerable format of a book that can be made to look like other books on the shelf. Yet, he says that he will preserve it from all mechanical and human distortions of any substance as it passes through the mechanical and human processes of duplication.

Let's face it. If he is truly the God of all creation, he can manage a publishing venture. No trick at all to protect his message from contamination. But why would God stoop to such an ordinary medium of expression? Couldn't the omnipotent Creator of the universe reveal himself to us in the marvels of nature? In the providential turns of human history? In the nobility and moral consciousness of the inner nature?

He certainly does. But in none of these sources does God make himself known to us in such concrete and explicit terms as in this written revelation. And here's why: the message—all of it—happens to be about a Person, a Person we need to know intimately. We need a body of literature that will give us detailed description, reasoned analysis, historical fact, poetic inspiration, and trustworthy predictions in order to acquaint us with such a Person. It's because of him that this is the world's most controversial Book, because he is the world's most controversial Person.

That's what this message is all about—God in human flesh. The written Word calls him the living Word. And, after all, what better way is there to preserve the spoken word than in the form of a book? What more effective route can be found to the brain with knowledge than through the written word?

Spoken words are absorbed by the human brain at a rate of about 150 words per minute—the speed at which most of us talk. But written words can be absorbed at a rate of about 1,500 words per minute. This means graphic communication is superior as far as speed of learning and prolonged retention of information are concerned. The psychologists estimate that approximately 90 percent of all we learn comes into the brain through the eye. God knew what he was doing when he recorded the Word.

The Bible, because of the very fact that it is to all outward appearances just one of the world's many, many books, pulls us into the very center of the conflict between doubt and faith. But, actually, it isn't the Bible that's at the heart of our trouble—it's that Person. Think about it for a moment. The record says that if you stumble at the Bible it is because you stumble at the one revealed in the Scriptures as God incarnate. Jesus Christ, who is described as "the express image of God," becomes "a rock of offense, even to them which stumble at the word" (1 Pet. 2:8).

You can't separate the written Word from the living Word. It's all one report, one gospel—a physical, yet a spiritual phenomenon. This message from God, about God, is humanly manufactured in the sense that it is produced in the shape of a book, yet it is divinely sponsored and authored. Thus, it is both naturally and supernaturally placed in my path and in yours, to become either a stone of stumbling or a rock of security.

Either God means what he says or he doesn't. "Behold, I lay . . . for a foundation a stone, a tried stone, a precious corner stone, a sure foundation: he that believeth shall not make haste" (Isa. 28:16).

A hasty reaction will judge what we say as an over-simplification, but I am convinced that this is where the action is, that this Word of God is where most faith begins to operate or most doubts begin to incubate. Take your time. Just one easy little step—"I will believe that the Bible is God speaking." All it amounts to is yielding to his terms this time, in the place of your own. His terms: "He that is of God heareth God's words" (John 8:47).

The Bible demands it, and there's no simpler, no more reasonable way to begin to walk away from doubt.

2.
A MATTER OF
COMMUNICATION

If your religion hasn't changed your life, you'd better change your religion.

For those who have not broken step with us since the preceding chapter, one thing has been made clear: the problem of doubt is a communication problem. What we decide to do with the written message called the Bible is the starting point in the whole process of putting doubts to rest.

The act of communication is usually considered to be complete when there is (1) a communicator, or sender; (2) a communicatee, or receiver; and (3) a message. But such an arrangement suggests a mechanical, one-way process. True communication is reciprocal; to be complete and effective, it requires a fourth ingredient: response.

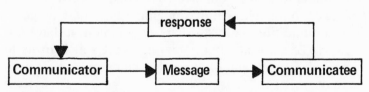

The whole purpose in communicating is to produce a response, to affect behavior, to change attitudes. Otherwise,

27

why would advertisers in this country spend in the neigh-
borhood of twenty billion dollars each year? They have
but one objective in paying so much for their communication, and that is to create a favorable response
toward their products or services—specifically, to stimulate
sales.

The conductor of an orchestra communicates by gestures
in order to get a reaction from his trained musicians. The
military officer communicates verbally to his inferiors to
see his orders obeyed. The movie scriptwriter, the novelist,
the playwright—all communicate through their chosen
media for the purpose of moving an audience to one
emotion or another.

All our communication normally is calculated to produce
action on the part of others. The behavior principle can't
be left out of our definition, because all effective communication depends upon some sort of response.

The original communicator is God. "He who calls" is
one of the basic meanings his name connotes. God has
called to every member of the human race in one way
or another since the birth of mankind. He is the sender;
the Bible is his message; man is his intended receiver.

And like every true communicator, God generates sig-
nals for a purpose. He wants to influence our behavior.
He wants to change our lives. He created us in the first
place to have fellowship with him (the oldest usage of
"communication" was "to share in common; to have fellowship"). He sends out a message that will help us to
know about him, and discover that he has a plan for each
one of us.

To do this, he uses the same thing that we use to communicate with each other—words. This is how it all started:

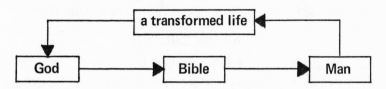

"In the beginning was the Word, and the Word was with God, and the Word was God" (John 1:1).

His message tells us that he actually spoke the universe into existence. In his ancient book of beginnings, Genesis, you'll find the phrase "and God said" used ten times in the opening chapter. As you explore further you will find God speaking to the first man, Adam; to the preserver of life, Noah; to the father of a race, Abraham; to civilization's lawgiver, Moses. He spoke to selected judges, to kings, and to prophets.

He spoke in different times, in different tongues, in different ways. And he "hath in these last days spoken unto us by his Son" (Heb. 1:2). We have to remind ourselves that the written Word is about the Word made flesh. This means that God's revelation of himself reaches its perfection in the person of Jesus Christ, whose surname is the Logos.

When Democritus described words as "the shadows of actions," he gave us a definition that is not only graphic but precise. What is a word but the expression of an idea conceived in the mind? When the incarnation was conceived in the mind of God—a living Word to make men free—then what better way to foretell it and to describe it than in the marvelous before-the-fact promises of the Old Testament followed by the sensational after-the-fact news reports of the New Testament? The ultimate unveiling of God to man is through something called "the Word."

You Can Believe It

This places the Bible in exactly the right perspective. It is not the supreme revelation, marvelous as it is. It points us to the supreme revelation, Christ. Man is not to worship a Bible, but the Person revealed in the Bible. Christianity is not the religion of a book, but the religion of a Person.

Neither is the Bible the exclusive method by which God has revealed himself. He has used other avenues of revelation beside the printed word. As the Bible itself remarks, "The heavens declare the glory of God; and the firmament sheweth his handywork" (Ps. 19:1). The intricacy and the magnitude of the discoverable world of nature are direct testimony of his infinite intelligence and awesome power. But despite its grandeur, this revelation from the natural universe doesn't tell us all that we need to know about God.

Also through the inner nature, whether we call it the psyche, the soul, or—more particularly—the conscience, God has revealed himself to each of us in undeniable and individual terms. Because of this conscious moral nature, we find it impossible to disclaim an awareness of him; or to avoid a guilt feeling when our lives are out of communication (out of fellowship) with God. That happens to be the way he made us.

When people volitionally suppress the truth of God that comes to them by these routes of the natural environment and the inner revelation, their so-called ignorance of him then takes on a deliberate character. The Bible says very frankly of the heathen, "they did not like to retain God in their knowledge" (Rom. 1:28). They willed to reject the testimony of the natural world about them, as well as the voice that spoke through conscience. The result was that they established their own religious systems.

Archaeology, discovering the same truth which the Bible teaches, assures us that, according to the earliest records, man was first a monotheist. He trusted in a single God, and gave evidence of an instinctive knowledge of right and wrong. Primitive people of every society, even without the special revelation bestowed on the Hebrew tribes, demonstrated by their conduct that they possessed this knowledge to a degree. As this rudimentary revelation was rejected by choice, polytheistic religions and worship of idols evolved in nation after nation.

In our artificial environment of today, this proclivity for recognizing God in the phenomena of nature is undoubtedly dulled. The hardware of our society and the degree of sophistication which we have attained tend to make the world of nature remote to a people who look more to electricity and medicine and automation than to God.

But civilized man can move toward animalism, idolatry, savagery, and immorality as he denies the presence of God in his universe—external and internal—just as primitive man could. And how much more deliberate his departure becomes if he also chooses to neglect and distrust the written message that was not available to primitive man!

No Better Record Available

It is clear to us, then, that God has revealed himself at sundry times and in different ways. The climax of revelation came almost twenty centuries ago when God actually inhabited human flesh for about thirty-three years. Today, the most complete disclosure we have is the written record of all these revelations, including that mysterious incarnation.

This is why God's Word is the inescapable starting place for the clearing away of all doubts. It wraps up for us all of God's redemptive acts in nature, in the heart of man and in history. First, he revealed himself to the people. This divine preferment crystallized into a nation apart, the "chosen race" of Israel. Next, the people, under the compulsion of God's own Spirit, produced the book.

Wait a minute, you say. What's that about the Hebrews and divine inspiration? If this book was produced by the minds and hands of Semitic people, then what keeps it from being just an anthology of Hebrew literature?

That's a fair question. But let me say the same thing: wait just a minute or so until we get into the next chapter. But for right now, regardless of what you (as a Jew or as a Gentile) think of that ancient race, let's allow the record to speak to the same question. "What advantage then hath the Jew? . . . Much every way; chiefly, because that unto them were committed the oracles of God" (Rom. 3:1-2).

Remember our agreement: "I will believe that the Bible is God speaking." That means we do not believe that it is man speaking. But God worked through human instrumentalities to bring his Word into existence through that marvelous process we call the inspiration of the Scriptures. Have you noticed the order in which all this came about? It's important: first the Word, then the life, then the literature.

The Bible is aptly referred to sometimes as "the word of life," because its purpose is not merely to inform, like so many books, but to redeem. The need of man is not just for information, but for salvation from a hopeless condition in which he finds himself. The Bible's job is to inform us of a Redeemer who is able to accomplish the more important task.

If you never understand the Bible fully, don't let that bother you, because it will work for you if you believe it without fully understanding it. It is belief, not knowledge, that makes all the difference. An intellectual who made this remarkable discovery for himself once wrote: "I am not ashamed of the gospel of Christ: for it is the power of God unto salvation to every one that believeth. . . . For therein is the righteousness of God revealed" (Rom. 1:16-17).

We need to recognize right here the fact that doubt is only partly intellectual—perhaps that's the smallest part. Doubt is largely volitional. It's not that we can't understand, in every instance. Likely as not, we simply don't want to understand. We develop a fondness for our own pet doubts.

But the ugly truth must also be faced that doubts are emotional fixtures as well as intellectual and volitional exercises. The old term "redoubtable" reminds us of the blood kinship that links doubt and fear. Just ask any psychiatrist about the psychosomatic linkage between emotional insecurity and sickness.

Now let's tackle those doubts about whether the Bible is inspired literature.

3.
THE MESSAGE THAT BREATHES

The worst of men would not have written the Bible; the best of men could not have written it.

The one thing that makes the Bible the touchstone of our faith is the fact that it is unlike any other book in the world. It is unique in its claim to be the revealed message of God to man. For such a claim to be believable, there would have to be convincing evidence that the book is inspired—actually breathed upon by the Spirit of God so that it becomes a living Word in a very real sense.

Inspiration, then, is the critical issue, the test of our credulity. If "the prophecy came not in old time by the will of man: but holy men of God spake as they were moved by the Holy Ghost" (2 Pet. 1:21), then we can accept it gladly. Our position is secure: "God said it; therefore, I believe it."

But can we determine to our satisfaction that God literally inspired the writing of the Bible? We don't want our acceptance to be on any footing that affronts intelligence or common sense.

There are people, you know, who want the Bible around because they may be afraid not to have one nearby. Such people are frequently unacquainted with its contents, but they have a respect for it which borders on superstition.

There can be no trace of fear, no compromise with critical thought, no fanciful rationalization in our acceptance. We know there is no magic involved here, and we're not interested in illusion.

But here's where the unique character of the Bible begins to manifest itself. The most profound thinkers delight in studying this work, because it challenges intellect in a thousand areas. For the curious, the Bible is beyond question one of the world's most interesting fact-books. Its pages are crammed with chunks of history, biography, poetry, philosophy, adventure. Its subject matter ranges widely over science, jurisprudence, psychology, architecture, warfare, astronomy, agriculture, ethnology, hygiene, astrology—you name it. And yet it makes no claim at all to being such a compendium.

A good deal of what the world knows about a good many things can be traced back to this reservoir of human knowledge. As William Lyon Phelps observed: "Our civilization is founded upon the Bible. More of our ideas, our wisdom, our philosophy, our literature, our art, our ideals come from the Bible than from all other books put together." It is a monumental cultural achievement admired by intellectuals—whether they accept its teachings or not.

Thomas Henry Huxley, for example, is credited with inventing the word *agnostic*. But he confesses: "Take the Bible as a whole, make the severest deductions which fair criticism can dictate for shortcomings and positive errors . . . and there still remains in this old literature a vast residuum of moral beauty and grandeur." A backhanded compliment from a doubter, but respect for the Bible as an intellectual work, nevertheless.

And Frederic Harrison, an exponent of positivism, concedes that "the English Bible is the true school of English literature. It possesses every quality of our language in its highest form." The list of those who admired the Bible from a distance can be extended—Goethe, Macaulay, Stevenson, Rousseau, Whitman, Darwin, Clemens.

But the Bible, we say, is different from any other book. It demands more than superstition, rationalization, or intellectual admiration. It requires not that we approve it or disapprove it, but that we accept it on faith as the inspired word of God—or reject it utterly. No middle position is left open to us. We aren't permitted the privilege of taking parts of it as God-inspired and leaving out parts of it as man-motivated.

Do you see the issue clearly? Either it is God's message to the world or it is not. If it is, then we can trust it with our very lives. If it is not, it deserves no more attention than *Pilgrim's Progress* or *Paradise Lost* or any other work of man produced by dedicated and conscientious effort.

If It's Proof You Want

The question confronting us is desperately important. How do we know this book is inspired? Suppose you have "honest" doubts and you sit down before the open Bible. You even pray, "Lord, I believe; help Thou mine unbelief." Does God help? Are there any evidences you can turn to that prove unmistakably the inspiration of the Bible?

Yes, there are. Let's review some of them.

1. *Its ideals.* Compare the doctrines of the Bible with

those you find in the Koran, the Code of Hammurabi, the writings of Confucius, the best of classic philosophy, or any other literature of nobility. You will not find in them such a loftiness of teachings about justice, the sacredness of human life, the sanctity of the home, the religious equality of the sexes, the concept of freedom as a human birthright, the dimensions of love, the beauty of holiness, or the assurance of hope. If you will persistently study its objectives, you will have to come to the conviction that the Bible's majestic aims far exceed the ideals of human authorship.

2. *Its efficacy.* It can be demonstrated without question that the Bible has played an historic role in the rise and fall of nations. In "A Study of History," Arnold Toynbee marshals documentary evidence of the correlation between God's Word and the advances of Western civilization over the world's less enlightened societies. Even today, the news media refer to those areas of the globe where the Bible message has taken root as the "Free World."

On the more observable personal level, no other book has transformed individual lives as this one has in every century since the canon was completed. Martyrdom would be a negligible factor in history if it were not for the uncounted millions who took their stand on the fundamental truths and promises proclaimed in this book.

Don't sell all these people short. Could your life be transformed by anything less than a spiritual provocation? Would it be logical to pretend that man-made propaganda could affect human behavior so profoundly in the fourth century and again in the seventh and the twelfth and the sixteenth and the nineteenth and, yes, the twentieth centuries? Divine inspiration would have to supply the impetus.

3. *Its integrity.* The Bible is completely honest. Literarians marvel at the purity of its style and have attempted to imitate its simple, direct way of communicating profound truths. For some, the imitation has been an effort to improve one's own effectiveness as a writer, but for a few others, the purpose has been to fabricate spurious Scriptures which would throw doubt on the Bible's integrity. Oddly, every venture at counterfeiting has been exposed, and the imitations have remained just that.

If you want an idea of how boldly the Bible lays itself open to textual criticism, notice how many details the Greek physician Luke, writing under inspiration, crowds into one brief passage: "Now in the fifteenth year of the reign of Tiberius Caesar, Pontius Pilate being governor of Judaea, and Herod being tetrarch of Galilee, and his brother Philip tetrarch of Ituraea, and of the region of Trachonitis, and Lysanias the tetrarch of Abilene, Annas and Caiaphas being the high priests, the word of God came unto John the son of Zacharias in the wilderness" (Luke 3:1-2).

Here is a reporter packing fifteen seemingly irrelevant details into his narrative which can easily be checked out for verification or proof of error. A man who writes like this exposes himself to all kinds of possibility for factual inaccuracy. Wouldn't it have been safer simply to leave out some of the data? Luke's account would have read just as smoothly without including any of these items of information.

But they are included, and they correspond perfectly with historical documentation. If the Bible were not a stickler for detail and accuracy, its believability would have

been damaged long ago. Think of the embarrassing, ludicrous errors in some of the Greek and Roman accounts
of creation. The stories are so far-fetched they have been
long since dismissed as fanciful mythology.

Can you cite with authority a single discrepancy in this
book written before the dawn of scientific knowledge? With
the moon-shaking discoveries of this enlightened age, why
has not even one grotesque mistake been found in the
Bible report—some monstrous error that would shake the
composure of millions of believers?

There's just one answer: the Bible is what it claims to
be—the inerrant Word of God, inspired in a sense that
applies to no other book.

4. *Its composition.* About forty persons from at least
seven countries, over a span of 1,600 years, were chosen
to take creative dictation from the Holy Spirit. Consider
the lack of preparation for literary achievement of such
unlikely prospects as Peter, a fisherman; Amos, a nur-
seryman; Joshua, a professional soldier; David, a shepherd
lad; Matthew, a tax collector; or Micah, a peasant.

A few wrote from the advantaged position of king or
priest or lawyer, but most of the writers of these sixty-six
books were unlettered laborers, farmers, prisoners, herds-
men. Could such a motley assemblage of contributors be
expected to pen portions of a cohesive literary work that
would survive generations of criticism?

As one of 57 co-authors in a jointly-produced college
textbook venture, I know what I'm talking about. It was
considered a good work and was widely used for a decade
(a reasonable life span for today's books). But I am frank
to admit that its chapter arrangement and sporadic presen-
tations of concepts achieved about as much coherence as

a procession of freight cars in a mile-long train.

It isn't reasonable to assume a consistency of style and purpose and orderly revelation in a collaboration of this sort. And when you're confronted by writing from forty sources—from different nationalities and from different centuries—you would logically expect some gross disharmony in the finished product. Yet the Bible hangs together as if it bore the imprint of a single hand—which it does.

5. *Its indestructibility.* Like hammers that wear themselves out on an everlasting anvil, the critics have come and gone while the Bible awaits the pounding of the next in line. The labored writings of Jeremiah were personally destroyed by the penknife and hearth fire of an arrogant king called Jehoiakim. The king's life and work have been forgotten by the world, but the inspired words of Jeremiah are very much in circulation today.

A spiteful Voltaire predicted in 1778 that the Bible would pass from common use within one hundred years. Less than twenty-five years after his death, Voltaire's home was being used as headquarters for a Bible society which has distributed more than 400 million copies of the "doomed" book since his prediction. Today, 25 million copies of the Bible are bought annually. Who reads Voltaire except students assigned to the task?

The misguided Englishman who became for awhile a fiery American patriot, Thomas Paine, said proudly after his all-out attack on God's Word: "I have now gone through the Bible, as a man would go through a wood with an ax, and felled trees. Here they lie, and the priests may replant them, but they will never make them grow." What's the world's bestseller today—Paine's *Age of Reason* or the Bible?

In spite of book burnings, calculated mistranslations, the ravages of time, human carelessness, and organized institutional opposition, the Bible has survived. Its message is available right now in 1,473 languages—and in such obscure dialects as Kung, Nama, Mao Naga, Ogoni, and Kekchi—which makes it the world's most widely translated literature. Efforts by the Communist world to get the briefest extracts of Lenin into as many tongues have failed miserably.

God said "Heaven and earth shall pass away, but my words shall not pass away" (Matt. 24:35). You've got to admit he's been right all this time.

6. *Its foreknowledge.* Industrial engineer G. B. Hardy, in a remarkable little book, asks the same question we're contemplating: "Has God 'touched' the Bible? Does it bear His fingerprint? What can prove His touch? . . . But one thing . . . FOREKNOWLEDGE. Only the supernatural mind can have prior knowledge to the natural mind. If then the Bible has foreknowledge, historical and scientific, beyond the permutation of chance . . . it truly then bears the fingerprint of God. If the Bible bears his fingerprint, surely then we can trust it. Surely we would be fools to ignore it." [1]

Without straining for artificial harmonization or unreal analogies, we can cite hundreds of specific scientific and historical events foretold in the pages of the Bible—events otherwise unreported or undiscovered until later centuries or indeed, the last few decades. For example, the literal restoration of Israel in 1948 is hinted in Isaiah 11; Jeremiah 33; Ezekiel 11; and Amos 9. The twentieth-century world war syndrome is described in Luke 21. The accelerated increase in knowledge in the "last days" is mentioned in

Daniel 12:4. The specter of nuclear fission is graphically foretold in 2 Peter 3:12. The prescientific announcement of the hydrologic cycle theory appears in Job 36:27-29; Psalm 135:7; and Ecclesiastes 1:6-7.

For a convincing as well as interesting demonstration of the astounding foreknowledge revealed in earlier portions of the Scripture, consult one of the editions of the Bible which key the messianic prophecies found in the Old Testament. You will find more than 300 minutely detailed predictions in the ancient books of law and history and poetry and prophecy, along with their precise fulfillment in the New Testament of the first century. The birth, the life, the ministry, the trial, the crucifixion, the burial, and the resurrection of Jesus Christ are announced centuries in advance of their occurrence, including such minutiae as the fact that a few Roman soldiers would shoot dice at the foot of the cross for the Nazarene's only earthly possession, a robe.

Such tests of the Bible's foreknowledge open up a fascinating territory for exploration which we will pursue in a later chapter. For now, we want only to make the point that the secrets of the ages are locked up in this mysterious book and that they are revealed to us in successive stages as the Spirit of God wills. It would require inspiration for mere words to be impregnated with such a power.

It's a Sure Thing

This one thing is certain. To say that the Bible is an inspired book is to say that it is a spiritual book. If the human authors needed the Holy Spirit's enablement in the writing of the Scriptures, then we need the same assistance if we are to read it with understanding.

The Bible itself tells us the same thing: "Which things also we speak, not in the words which man's wisdom teacheth, but which the Holy Ghost teacheth; comparing spiritual things with spiritual. But, the natural man receiveth not the things of the Spirit of God: for they are foolishness to him; neither can he know them, because they are spiritually discerned" (1 Cor. 2:13-14).

Which takes us back to our starting position: the root of doubting, for most of us today, is buried in our attitude toward the Bible. We can't even read it intelligently unless we approach it with spiritual discernment and an unquestioning faith in its veracity as the inspired word of God.

Once we get past that point, the path ahead is less obscure, and we begin to find light for the next step.

-----

[1] From *Countdown* by G. B. Hardy (Chicago: Moody Press, Moody Bible Institute of Chicago, 1967), p. 28. Used by permission.

4.
A HEAVENLY GIFT IN EARTHLY VESSELS

Question the divine inspiration of Scripture and
you have only good advice—the Bible is not good
advice, but "good news."

How does an "inspired" writer function? In what manner
does the revelation come to him? Is he aware that the
words he writes are really God's words?

God's ways are past defining, of course. But he allows
us a stimulating glance of how his chosen writers worked.
It was very much the way any other writer works. They
had a message; they thought about it; they wrote it out;
and they wondered about what they had written.

The essential difference is that the inspired authors of
the Bible were used by the Lord to preserve a portion
of the revealed message, whether they understood the full
significance of all the words or not.

Whether God appeared to them in "visions" or "the-
ophanies" or whatever, he spoke to them in such a way
that they understood the urgency and the grandeur of the
role they were called upon to play. And he did not oblit-
erate their personalities, but allowed them full expression
as conveyors of his communication.

It is fascinating to explore the personal thoughts and
feelings of some of the men who were partners to this

supernatural collaboration. They reacted in varying fashions to the divine compulsion.

Job, for example, seemed to be laboring under the burden of his calling when he exclaimed: "Oh that my words were now written! oh that they were printed in a book!" (Job 19:23). Then, as though musing on the vulnerability of scrolls and books for so precious a message, he added: "That they were graven with an iron pen and lead in the rock for ever!" (Job 19:24). Finally Job overcomes his worrying with this conclusion: "For I know that my redeemer liveth, and that he shall stand at the latter day upon the earth: and . . . in my flesh shall I see God" (Job 19:25-26).

In other words, with a terrific burst of faith in the providence of God and the resurrection promise, Job is saying to himself, "It may not seem to be a durable record, but if the Lord puts it on my heart to write it down, I know that he will be able to take care of this message in the exact form in which he transmits it to me."

From his faraway setting in the ghetto of Babylon, the exiled Ezekiel penned one of the most complicated and intriguing books of the Bible. He hardly fails to begin every chapter with the same credential: "The word of the Lord came unto me, saying. . . ."

And look at the charming personality of the disciple John beaming through this testimony: "This is the disciple which testifieth of these things, and wrote these things: and we know that his testimony is true. And there are also many other things which Jesus did, the which, if they should be written every one, I suppose that even the world itself could not contain the books that should be written" (John 21:24-25).

How could an amanuensis under the direction of the Holy Spirit more clearly inform us of the manner in which he was being used than Jeremiah does? He says simply, "The word that came to Jeremiah from the Lord, saying, Thus speaketh the Lord God of Israel, saying, Write thee all the words that I have spoken unto thee in a book" (Jer. 30:1-2).

In his first letter to the Corinthians, Paul reveals how his own reflective thought processes function uninhibitedly even while under the influence of the Holy Spirit. Writing on the delicate matter of conjugal morality, Paul says: "And unto the married I command, yet not I but the Lord" (1 Cor. 7:10), and then proceeds with a reference to actual instructions spoken by Jesus in Matthew 5:32; in Mark 10:11; and in Luke 16:18 on the subject of separation of man and wife.

Paul then adds: "But to the rest speak I, not the Lord" (1 Cor. 7:12), because he is clearly no longer quoting the words of Jesus. There is no question of inspiration here, but rather an expression of awareness on Paul's part of the difference that exists between the commandments of Christ on the matter and the related area left open to the exercise of each individual's judgment. This is clarified a few verses later where Paul writes: "Now concerning virgins I have no commandment of the Lord: yet I give my judgment" (1 Cor. 7:25).

To quote just one more personality, the rough fisherman who beforehand probably lacked the ability to write his own name was spiritually empowered to give us this eloquent assurance: "Knowing this first, that no prophecy of the scripture is of any private interpretation. For the prophecy came not in old time by the will of man: but

holy men of God spake as they were moved by the Holy
Ghost" (2 Pet. 1:20-21).

Peter speaks here with authority that has an eternal ring
to it. Where in the world did he acquire it? He got it,
of course, from outside of this world.

If you think it takes credulity on your part to trust in
God's ability to preserve his message, just visualize for
a moment the faith required of all those who first wrote
it down. While they scribed these fragile scrolls, God gave
to them the calm expectation that their words would somehow stand as long as the earth lasts. You and I are in
a position, from this end, to see that God hasn't so far
failed one of these prophetic voices.

Still, doesn't it seem strange that the most urgent message
of all time comes to us in one of the flimsiest packages
imaginable? A mere book can be mutilated or destroyed
with very little effort. It has to be reprinted just in order
to avoid becoming extinct. It is subject to the innocent
mistake of the copyist or typographer, and to the deliberate
tampering of the translator or interpreter.

After all, is a book, bought and sold in the marketplace
like other consumer items, the best medium for recording
and preserving the voice of God? The answer is, obviously,
yes. Otherwise, God would not have chosen written communication.

It's Easy to Believe

Actually, the process by which the Bible has come to
us is the most natural unfolding of God's revelation
blended with the evolution of the history of writing. A
smoother flow of the inspired message from the beginning
to now could not be imagined.

Until recently, scholars were somewhat bothered by the opinion that writing was not known in the time of Moses, who was perhaps the first inspired writer of Scripture, around 1500 B.C. The Bible teaches that inspired writing did indeed begin with Moses. As a matter of fact, the "experts" disagree over the authorship of the five books of Moses, as they do over other portions of the Bible. They point to the interweaving of three documents in the books of Moses which they label the J, E, and P texts, and which they believe to be produced by separate sources. You may wish to spend time investigating for yourself the tiresome debates of the textual authorities, but there is no evidence that supersedes or improves on the record itself:

"And the Lord said unto Moses, Write this for a memorial in a book" (Ex. 17:14).

"And Moses wrote all the words of the Lord" (Ex. 24:4).

"And the Lord said unto Moses, "Write thou these words" (Ex. 34:27).

"And thou shalt write upon them all the words of this law" (Deut. 27:3).

"When Moses had made an end of writing the words of this law in a book, until they were finished" (Deut. 31:24).

Remember, God has never given any indication that the preservation of his message would be dependent on scholarship or human knowledge. To the contrary he promised that he would preserve it "by the power of his own might." As impressive as knowledge is, it is powerless in the work of redemption unless faith is operative.

Conviction in the heart can accomplish what information in the brain can't even begin. As Stuart Mill put it, "One man with a belief has more force than one hundred with an interest."

And later discoveries in archaeology have yielded evidence that writing was in use even before the time of Moses. The primitive Canaanites—long before they were overrun by the invading Hebrew tribes whom Moses had led out of bondage in Egypt—had a written language which was the direct ancestor of the Phoenician alphabet we depend on today.

The first writing that was found in great quantities was in the form of pictographs, carved or printed on the tombs and buildings and pottery of ancient Egypt. These were hybrid forms which were partly writing, partly drawing.

Next came cuneiform, or "nail-shaped" writing, in which the characters were pressed into soft clay by a wedge-like instrument. Thousands of portable clay tablets have been dug out of the ruins of the great cities of Mesopotamia, like Babylon and Ur. These specimens include gargantuan postcards of clay on which private correspondence and business statements were recorded.

Papyrus provided a leap forward and gave us the word from which *paper* was to be derived. The Egyptians produced this breakthrough in technique by pressing and drying the inner bark of a water plant resembling sedge. They rolled the thin bark into continuous sheets almost half the length of a football field. With such scrolls, prolonged portions of writing could now be preserved safely simply by rolling them up and storing them in tightly-closed jars.

Undoubtedly Moses and his successors made use of papyrus in recording the messages that came to them by divine inspiration. After all, he had spent eighty years of his life in Egypt, which was now exporting papyrus all over the known world as the craft of writing became more widespread. The classics of Greek literature were originally written on the same material.

But as technology marched onward (at a snail's pace), papyrus was eventually replaced by skins, which proved to be far more durable. In damp climates, for instance, papyrus had a tendency to rot, and for this reason all of the original manuscripts of the Bible disappeared.

The first animal to fall victim to the new industry was the calf, whose skin was peculiarly suitable for rendering into extremely durable sheets of vellum. Later parchment, made from sheepskin, became the preferred medium. The oldest Bible manuscripts that we have today are copies made on vellum or parchment from the original papyrus rolls.

At long last, books replaced the rolls. They first appeared in Rome in the third century. As you might expect, these books started out as not much more than sheets of parchment stacked in a certain order and carried about in a leather bag. Then permanent covers fashioned of oak and leather were bound onto the pages themselves, into what the Romans called "codexes," because one of the first books to appear was the Latin code, or law.

Breakthrough in Communication

By the time bookmaking had evolved into a highly decorative art in the Middle Ages, the greatest technical stride of all was on the threshold of discovery. An inventive German craftsman named Johann Gutenberg was about to give the world mechanical printing.

Paper, ink, and even metal printing plates had been developed earlier in the Orient. But when Gutenberg's slip of a knife—a sheer accident which spoiled a whole printing plate he was carving out—caused a single character of the alphabet to drop on the floor and thus give him the idea of movable, interchangeable type, the age of modern mass communication was born.

Historians ever since haven't been sure whether the printing press was a creature of the so-called industrial revolution or, what is more likely, the creator of it. Gutenberg has been labeled by one contemporary authority as "the father of all assembly lines."

What we do know is that this new process of machine-duplicated communication immediately began to transform society because it revolutionized Bible manufacturing. Just as it began to circulate the intellectual output of the Renaissance in all directions, so did it publish the great arguments of the Protestant Reformation in all enlightened countries.

It is significant that the press was carried westward by the tides of human history rather than eastward; for example, printing didn't get across the Carpathian Mountains into Russia for a century and a half—neither did the Reformation movement. And some historians have felt that without the incendiary pamphlets which so effectively galvanized public opinion, there would not have been either a French or an American revolution.

It is also significant that one of the first things printed was the famous Gutenberg Bible, of which only 47 are now in existence. One of these was recently offered for sale by a New York book dealer at the modest price of $2,750,000.

What all this means to you is that the Bible you hold in your hand today has come through a transformation as old as history itself. If there's a question lurking in the shade, let's turn the light of honest inquiry on it. How can we be sure, if all the originals are missing, that the copies we now have say the same things the very first inspired manuscripts said?

To rephrase what may be a nagging doubt for some, how reliable are the copies of the sixty-six books of the Old Testament and the New Testament which have come down to us over many centuries and through many changes in handwriting and materials and mechanical processes? It's a sensible question. And there's a sensible answer.

For one thing, we know a lot about the copying methods used. We have an abundance of documentary information on how the professional scribes went about their task. No apprentice was admitted to the practice until he had completed a lengthy period as an understudy. After all, this was one of the few specialized vocations open to the few prepared for something other than common labor, and was regarded more highly than medicine or law up to the time of Christ.

The work of a scribe was unbelievably exacting. In the case of Scripture, the copyist went through the ritual beforehand of taking a complete bath in order not to add any foreign element to the sacred page. And each time he prepared to write the word for *Lord*, he wiped his pen clean as a gesture of the utmost dedication to the demands of his assignment.

As a thoroughly practical safeguard, the scribe was trained to first count every word in the manuscript about to be copied. Then he counted each letter, and jotted down the totals. Next he set to work, using thread to insure straight lines across the page, much as a bricklayer follows his leveling line. When he finished copying, he would again count the words and letters. If the totals didn't correspond precisely, the entire new manuscript was destroyed and begun all over.

No Shortage of Evidence

Keep in mind that there was really no need for copying the carefully preserved originals until several centuries had passed and the early papyrus manuscripts began to show signs of decomposition. As a result of such extreme care, there are nearly 4,500 known manuscripts of different portions of the Old Testament in existence, some dating back to A.D. 125. And when Jerome translated the complete Bible into Latin in A.D. 382, it is estimated that there were more than 35,000 copies of Old and New Testament books in circulation.

Compare this with only twelve copies of the works of Herodotus, the Greek historian. There are only nine or ten manuscripts of Caesar's "Gallic Wars" for scholars to check against each other—and the oldest one of these was recorded 900 years after Caesar wrote it. Yet, does anybody ever express any doubts about whether or not he's reading the real Julius Caesar?

To quote an authority, Professor John A. Scott says in his book, *Luke, Greek Physician and Historian,* "There is one great advantage which the New Testament can claim over all the writings of classical Greece, and that is the age and excellent condition of its manuscripts. Homer probably lived not far from 1000 B.C., yet the oldest manuscripts now extant containing the *Iliad* and the *Odyssey* are hardly older than the tenth century of the Christian era. Hence we see that almost two thousand years intervene between Homer and the oldest complete manuscript of his works which we possess.

"Most of the poetry of Pindar, who died about 450 B.C., has been lost, but the oldest manuscript of the poetry which has survived was written very near the year A.D. 1150. In other words, there is an interval of about 1600 years between Pindar and the date of his oldest manuscript.

"Demosthenes died in 322 B.C., while the oldest manuscript of any complete oration which we have is hardly earlier than A.D. 900. Those selected are the ones of which we have especially old and reliable manuscripts.

"With the New Testament we are in another world, for we have two manuscripts which were certainly written before 340, perhaps as early as A.D. 325. The New Testament probably received its final form about A.D. 100. Hence we have manuscripts of the New Testament which are removed from the compilation of that book by little more than two centuries, while in the case of the greatest writers of Greece, the average interval is more than eight times as great, or sixteen centuries . . .

"Well-meaning Christians often say that we must take the Gospels on faith. It takes about as much faith for me to believe the Gospels as it does for me to believe the binomial theorem or the multiplication table. Where knowledge enters, agnosticism flees." [1]

It is truly an amazing thing to realize that manuscript experts—believers and skeptics alike—have devoted lifetimes to studying, comparing, researching and double-checking these various copies of the message God bequeathed to the world. And no one yet has found anything to discredit the text. Other exciting archaeological finds—like the Babylonian Creation Stories, the Weld Prism, the Gil-

gamish Epic, some of which date from Abraham's time—
are recorded only on a single clay tablet or on a slab or
stone, without even one manuscript copy to offer a mini-
mum measure of corroboration.

The most recent discovery of worldwide dramatic impact, the Dead Sea Scrolls, was in 1947. One of these,
called St. Mark's Isaiah Scroll, contains the entire 66
chapters of Isaiah on excellently preserved parchment.
Surely now the Bible faced a real challenge, because tests
revealed the parchments to be at least 1,000 years older
than the Masoretic text of A.D. 916 to which our modern
Scripture is virtually identical.

Here's what Millar Burrows, the Yale professor of biblical theology who personally analyzed the scrolls, reported:
"Such agreement in a manuscript so much older gives
reassuring testimony to the general accuracy of the tradi-
tional text. . . . Herein lies its chief importance, supporting
the fidelity of the Masoretic tradition."

No substantial change in over 1,000 years! Is that evidence, or isn't it? And if one of the Dead Sea fragments
is Mark's Gospel, copied about A.D. 50—as an expert in
Rome's Pontifical Biblical Institute claims—then we have
one more startling piece of evidence of unchanging scriptural authenticity.

To be perfectly fair, and in the interest of clinical accuracy, it must be observed that some of the critics have
come up with "variations" in the existing texts of the Bible.
You may read sometime that there are as many as 180,000
variant readings. This sounds like a serious problem,
doesn't it?

However, all but about 400 of these variant readings
are minor differences like spelling *honor* with an "or" in

one manuscript and with "our" in another translation. Or like saying "to us ward" in one and changing it to "toward us" in another. These variations don't even remotely alter the sense of the message.

And of those 400 cases where you could say the sense of a passage is involved, not a single basic scriptural doctrine is at issue. These are purely linguistic or semantic variations which would be expected to occur in different dialects—especially when written at different dates in history after the language has had time to go through some idiomatic changes. You could accept any one of the readings without affecting any truth of the Bible.

Such special protection through centuries of copying and handling is convincing testimony that God has presided over the dissemination of his spiritual guidebook. And did you know that this is exactly what he said he would do? "So shall my word be that goeth forth out of my mouth: it shall not return unto me void, but it shall accomplish that which I please, and it shall prosper in the thing whereto I sent it" (Isa. 55:11).

---

[1] Quoted by Kenneth S. Wuest in *Great Truths to Live By from the Greek New Testament* (Grand Rapids: Wm. B. Eerdmans Publishing Company, 1952), p. 20. Used by permission.

5.
HOW DID THE BOOKS BECOME **THE BOOK?**

What the Bible needs today is fewer editors to revise it and more newsboys to deliver it.

The assembling of the sixty-six books of the Bible under one cover didn't just happen—or did it? Somewhere along the line, it would seem, decisions would have to be made about which books should be included and which should be rejected.

If such a measuring-stick was to be applied, who was qualified to wield it? If a "canon" was to be formed (the word comes from "cane" or "measuring rod") then who was to determine the standard by which God's Word would be authenticated? In the final analysis, only God himself could be expected to exercise such judgment, yet we have seen from the preceding discussion that the literal handling of the sacred material was committed to human hands.

Moses himself had ordered that the first five books—which the Hebrews called the Torah ("law") and the Greeks called the Pentateuch ("five books")—be placed in the ark within the tabernacle for safekeeping. For some time, this was all the Scripture available, but eventually the histories of the kings of Israel and Judah, the inspirational writings of David and Solomon, and the far-seeing books of the prophets were added.

All of these were carefully listed by Nehemiah and Ezra after the Babylonian captivity. It is an undisputed fact that the thirty-nine Old Testament books were all in place some 400 years before Christ and universally accepted by the Jews. The secular historian, Flavius Josephus, referring to the collection in the time of the Persian monarch, Artaxerxes, reported that "no one had dared up to his day, to add anything to them, to take anything from them, or to make any change in them."

These thirty-nine books fell under three main divisions: the law; the Hagiographa or "sacred writings" which we call the psalms; and the prophets. When Josephus compiled his list—the earliest nonbiblical accounting—he came up with the same number of books comprising "the law and the prophets and the psalms." This classification is confirmed by the words of Jesus: "And he said unto them, These are the words which I spake unto you, while I was yet with you, that all things must be fulfilled, which were written in the law of Moses, and in the prophets, and in the psalms concerning me" (Luke 24:44).

Jerome, one of the most astute scholars of the fourth century, found "the law, the prophets, and the Hagiographa" to be the complete contents of the Old Testament, and his examination of the documents convinced him there were exactly thirty-nine books. The Babylonian Talmud, which put the civil, ethical, and religious laws of the Jews in their most authoritative form two centuries after Jerome, is in precise agreement with the other sources.

Further indication that the Jewish canon was settled in the purposes of God appears in the conflict between Jesus and the scribes of his day. He repeatedly condemned the scribes, and the Pharisees as well, for interpreting the Scriptures to suit themselves. But never once did he accuse them of tampering with the text—a charge which he certainly would not have overlooked if it had been justified. God's Word was intact then, even if it was not being correctly applied.

I find the greatest assurance of all in the fact that Jesus Christ accepted the same Old Testament which we have. If you have any doubts about him, then of course you would question his testimony about the authenticity of the Bible. But if you will grant a plea of continuance, as a judge does to arguments he is yet to be convinced of, this doubt will be confronted in a later chapter where I believe you will be enabled to see how Jesus demonstrated that he was God in human flesh.

As God, he confirmed the Old Testament canon of his century in every respect. As God, he guaranteed that his words which were to be added to the existing canon would never pass away. As a matter of fact, he attaches to this matter the most deadly earnest warning: "For I testify unto every man that heareth the words of the prophecy of this book, If any man shall add unto these things, God shall add unto him the plagues that are written in this book"—and one of these plagues is doubt—"And if any man shall take away from the words of the book of this prophecy, God shall take away his part out of the book of life, and out of the holy city, and from the things which are written in this book" (Rev. 22:18-19).

For the Christian, then, the best test of canonicity is the self-verification pronounced by an incarnate God. "Search the scriptures," he encouraged believer and critic alike, for "they are they which testify of me" (John 5:39).

If he trusted the same Old Testament, if he quoted from it as the Word of God, if he raised no doubts of any kind about any portion of the message that has come down to us today, I can find no reason to question it. I can't speak for others, of course; but in my investigative research, I have not found a more reliable authority than Jesus of Nazareth.

The shaping up of the New Testament writings followed the same pattern. As the Holy Spirit pushed the martyr-spawning church across the hostile world of Jew and Greek and Roman during the first centuries of the gospel age, the inspired books of the New Testament were slowly added to the Hebrew canon.

The individual churches, hungry for the gospel and the letters of the apostles, were widely separated. Travel and communication were difficult, and Roman persecution was a grim fact of daily existence for the tiny groups of Christians throughout the mission field. Consequently, the earliest collections were incomplete. It was more than three centuries before all of the churches came into possession of copies of the four biographies or Gospels, Luke's volume of history called "The Acts of the Apostles," the twenty-one letters written by Paul and Peter and James and John and Jude, and the final work of John, the Revelation.

The same remarkable records of agreement began to appear in the fourth century in the form of catalogues prepared by early historians like Epiphanius, Augustine, Athanasius, Cyril, and Philaster. Six out of ten of these catalogues were in perfect agreement as to the New Testament canon. The other four were unsure about the authorship of Hebrews (which is still unknown), and uninformed about the last book of John.

The startling observation which we are in a position to make in this age is that God was able to steer his word past any conflicting human judgments. Where celebrated scholars of early times, like Origen or Eusebius or Irenaeus or Tertullian, couldn't see the whole picture, the final canon was never in jeopardy—because of divine supervision. The heroic Martin Luther, as late as the sixteenth century, might conscientiously object to the book of Esther as "heathenish" or to James as "a right strawy epistle." But he was powerless to affect the canonicity of either.

The point is that no single arbiter or delegated council ever had to sit down to pick and choose which books were the Lord's and which were man's. Oh, yes, there were councils which met—like the one in Carthage in A.D. 397 or in Trent in 1546. And they may have taken "official" action. But all that the ecclesiastical authorities really had any power to do was simply to approve the thirty-nine Old Testament books and the twenty-seven New Testament books that have come to us by God's providence.

The "Hidden" Writings

A most convincing demonstration of this is seen in the dramatic failure of human efforts to add to the Scripture the group of books known as the Apocrypha and to invest them with the same status as the books of the canon. These are "hidden" writings—the word *apocryphal* has come to mean "spurious, secret, of doubtful origin"—produced during the period of silence between the Old and the New Testaments.

Strictly speaking, the apocryphal books are approximately fourteen works which were added to the Old Testament by Jerome when he translated the Vulgate Bible.

He was compelled to make the additions by the clergy which had commissioned him to accomplish the translation from the earlier versions. Jerome, knowing that the Apocrypha was not a part of the Hebrew canon, made it clear that the books could be read "for edification" but could not be accepted as authoritative doctrine.

Martin Luther's translation of the canon into German in the sixteenth century also took exception to these extraneous books. He had them bound in the Bible between the Testaments with the observation: "These books are not held equal to the sacred scriptures, and yet are useful and good for reading."

Obviously, secular books can be stitched into the same format with God's Word, but even those denominations which have made this misstep have not been able to remove the "doubtful" label which stigmatizes these writings as counterfeit and no part of inspired Scripture. The Apocrypha, for all its value as contemporary literature, was never accepted by the Jews, was not once quoted by Jesus, was rejected by the early church, and has retained through the centuries—despite man's efforts—its identification as suspect literature.

The titles of the apocryphal books, which indeed have a "biblical sound," are as follows:

I Esdras
II Esdras
Tobit
Judith
The Rest of the Chapters of the Book of Esther
The Wisdom of Solomon
Ecclesiasticus

Baruch
The Song of the Three Holy Children
The History of Susanna
Bel and the Dragon
The Prayer of Manasses
I Maccabees
II Maccabees

Of these, the first book of the Maccabees is without controversy the most worthwhile reading, as it presents a colorful account of genuine historical value describing the rebellion of the Jews against the tyranny of the Seleucids and the brief period of national independence between 175 and 130 B.C. The books of Esdras and Manasses are questioned by some who accept the rest of the Apocrypha.

There were many more questionable writings produced as the literary output of the civilized world began to accelerate somewhat after the founding of the church. Especially as opposition to Christianity was mobilized, "pseudepigrapha" or fraudulent books, began to appear in number. At least fifty known forgeries were produced during the apostolic period. These fictions were given names that were rather patently mythical, such as:

The Gospel of the Egyptians
The Acts of Pilate
The Passing of Mary
Protevangelion of James
The Arabic Gospel of the Childhood
Letters of Paul to Seneca
The Shepherd of Hermas

The Apocalypse of Peter
The Gospel of Pseudo-Matthew
The Testament of the Twelve Patriarchs
The Secrets of Enoch

Such attempts at integrating legend with Scripture—and thus frustrating the whole direction of canonicity—were of no avail. The early churches accepted only those books which revealed immediate apostolic authority—those written by the apostles of Jesus or by those who shared directly in their ministry, such as Mark and Luke and Jude. Keep in mind that these various portions of the New Testament were making their appearance at widely separated locations—the Gospel of Luke first showed up in Greece, James in Palestine, Mark in Rome, 2 Peter in Asia Minor.

When the bitter Roman persecutions ended in the fourth century and the previously underground churches could begin to openly compare their collections, they discovered that just as God had presided over the survival of his church, he had shepherded the bringing together of his Word. The Apocrypha was branded, the pseudepigrapha were exposed, the respected "writings of the fathers" of the early church were recognized as being no more than helpful, informative documents, and the New Testament canon of twenty-seven books was closed.

Today, those who find it difficult to give credence to the power of divine preservation turn to the more sophisticated methods of ascertaining authenticity, namely historical criticism and textual criticism. Without involving ourselves in the methodology, let's see what the most modern investigative techniques tell us.

Under textual criticism, tedious laboratory testing is

conducted on actual handwriting, word usage, quality of papyrus or other material used, and age measurements. When subjected to such clinical scrutiny, a counterfeit "Epistle of Thomas" was found to be bound with the wrong kind of leather for the period in which it was supposedly produced. Later checking proved that the leather had been slyly removed from an old synagogue roll and attached to the fraudulent manuscript which some joker had hoped to pass off as the genuine article.

You may be sure that the Bible would not be standing today if the experts had not been able to come to agreement on which books belong. If any real divergence or discrepancy could be uncovered, modern scholarship would have set up before now a howl that couldn't be ignored. Even while we depend on the power of the Holy Spirit to protect the Bible, it is reassuring to find modern scientific authority corroborating our conviction.

How amazingly trustworthy is this expressive, coherent compendium of sixty-six books! Ages before, the Bible had said of itself: "The words of the Lord are pure words; as silver tried in a furnace of earth, purified seven times. Thou shalt keep them, O Lord, thou shalt preserve them from this generation for ever" (Ps. 12:6-7).

Language No Barrier

Just as amazing is the safe passage which the various books have made through the perilous waters of translation. The Bible itself exhibits several languages. Practically all of the Old Testament was written in Hebrew, and numerous words still remain intact in current translations, such as *selah, hosanna, amen,* and *cherubim.* The book of Daniel was recorded in Chaldee, the language of Babylon

where the prophet lived out his life as one of Nebuchadnezzar's specially trained linguists. Traces of the Chaldee
can still be found in the fateful "handwriting on the wall":
"MENE, MENE, TEKEL UPHARSIN" (Dan. 5:25),
which told Belshazzar he was weighed in the balances and
found wanting.

Even the Hebrews themselves couldn't understand their
own canon at the end of the 70-year Babylonian exile,
because Aramaic, a Hebrew-Syriac dialect, had replaced
the classical language in Palestine. Thus we read in the
eighth chapter of Nehemiah that the scribe Ezra made
a translation for the people into the common language
of their environment. When they read the freshly understandable Scripture, the record tells us that they were
moved to tears of repentance and a spiritual reformation
swept the entire nation.

The New Testament was recorded in *koine* Greek, the
vernacular established by the Hellenistic influences in
Palestine before the time of Christ. But Jesus himself spoke
the Aramaic dialect of his own people. Again we find traces
of the spoken tongue in phrases transferred bodily from
the Aramaic without translation, such as: *"Talitha cumi"*
(Mark 5:41), ("Damsel, I say unto thee, arise") and *"Eph-
phatha"* (Mark 7:34), ("be opened")—words which Jesus
spoke when reviving the child victim of a fever and when
opening the ears of a deaf mute. The most heart-rending
utterance that ever fell from the lips of Jesus was recorded
literally just as He cried it on the cross in his native language, *"Eli, Eli, lama sabachthani?"* (Matt. 27:46) ("My
God, my God, why hast thou forsaken me?")

Similarly, vestiges of the original Greek language appear
in today's English translations. Perhaps the best-known

example, occurring at least seventy-five times in the New Testament, is *baptizo,* a word which has no direct equivalent in English and which was therefore transliterated. Its inescapable signification in the Greek is "immerse," or "place into."

Another intriguing linguistic exhibit is found in Paul's statement: "If any man love not the Lord Jesus Christ, let him be Anathema Maranatha" (1 Cor. 16:22). Here we have an odd combination of untranslated terms drawn from two cultures: the Greek *anathema,* meaning "accursed"; and the Aramaic *maranatha,* which would be interpreted as "Our Lord will come."

It's not being suggested here that you have to be a language expert to read the Bible. But it might help to have an awareness of the fact that words do go through changes in the course of a few thousand years, and that the Bible, which covers a longer time span than any other book ever written, happens to document a number of such changes. Thus, with an understanding that the Scriptures provide a record of the evolution of language itself, there is no reason to be confused when you find a word appearing in many variant forms as it passes from the earliest Hebrew spelling through subsequent idioms. An example is the popular given name meaning "the Lord is salvation," which can be traced through the following eleven forms: Oshea, Joshua, Joshuah, Jeshua, Jeshuah, Jehoshua, Jehoshuah, Hosea, Hoshea, Osee, Jesus.

In the third century before Christ there was a translation of the Old Testament and of the apocryphal books into Greek. In honor of the seventy Jewish scholars of Alexandria who performed the task, the version was called the Septuagint ("the Seventy"). As long as Greek was the language of the civilized world, the Septuagint was the dominant translation.

By the third century after Christ, Latin had largely replaced Greek as the official language as the Roman Empire swallowed up Greek culture. There had been translations of the Bible into the Old Syriac and Coptic and Old Latin languages, but a new translation was now needed in the common or "vulgar" form of Latin being spoken everywhere. Therefore, when Jerome made his translation, known as the Vulgate, in the fourth century, the Scriptures appeared in the form in which they were to remain for almost 1,000 years.

During these ten centuries, usually considered as the Dark Ages, the light of the Bible was almost extinguished by an autocratic church hierarchy which came to consider the Vulgate its own property, not to be entrusted to the common people. Difficult as it may be to realize, possession of a copy of the Bible was a capital offense in some countries in the 1300's, and in sixteenth-century England, a law was passed stating that "no woman, no artificers, apprentices, servingmen, husbandmen, or laborers" should even be granted permission to read the church copy. The Dark Ages, indeed!

When Peter Waldo, a wealthy merchant in the Albi province of Southern France channeled all his personal resources into the translating of the gospel from the Latin into the language of his people in the twelfth century, such a revival of spiritual freedom swept across the lower regions of Europe that the reigning church lords of Rome redirected their Fifth Crusade, originally destined to wrest the Holy Land from the Turks, against Scripture-nurtured "heretics" in France. In that one purge alone, more than

200,000 "Waldenses" and "Albigenses" were massacred by the mercenary soldiers in the hire of the state church.

John Wycliffe took twenty-two years of his life to translate the whole Bible into English for the first time. His objective was to make the Bible "so any plowboy could understand," and the handmade copies of his 1395 translation sold for the equivalent of $2,000 each.

Thus the fires of enlightenment were already lit when Martin Luther undertook the staggering task of translating into the German language the original Hebrew and Greek documents—bypassing the Vulgate entirely. The Reformation was underway in earnest.

After William Tyndale produced the first machine-printed translation of the New Testament into English, that brought about his death by strangling and burning at the hands of the authoritarians who were enraged at the facility with which the Word of God was becoming the knowledge of all men, a flood of other translations followed: Coverdale's Bible, Matthew's Bible, the Great Bible, the Bishop's Bible, the Geneva Bible. The Dark Ages were over!

The People's Bible

Now the stage was set for the appearance in 1611 of the masterpiece of all translations up to that time—and, perhaps, of all time. Called the Authorized Version, but better known during the past three-and-a-half centuries as the King James Version, this has become the standard Bible for most Christians. Despite its seventeenth-century idiom, the King James Version has remained popular, and literary critics admit that the vigor and beauty of its expressive English have never been surpassed.

The King James Version is distinguished by the use of remarkably few words—a total vocabulary of about 6,000, as contrasted with about 20,000 in Shakespeare's works. And the words it favors are simple, direct, and short. It has been pointed out, for instance, that 80 percent of the words occurring in the Sermon on the Mount are of one syllable. Of 119 words in the twenty-third Psalm, 95 are monosyllabic. And review the 25 words used in the most famous Bible verse of all, John 3:16. You'll be surprised to see how much more expressive tiny words can be thān the four-dollar variety. The book of Mark is suggestive of the racy style of a modern news story, with a paucity of words of more than two syllables.

Other translations include the Rheims-Douai Bible of the same vintage as the King James. It was reissued in 1749 as the Challoner Revision, and has appeared in a modern version, the Confraternity Bible. The English Revised, the American Standard Revised, the Revised Standard Version, all new forms appearing during the past one hundred years, had access to manuscripts (labeled the Vatican, the Sinaitic, and the Alexandrian) not available to the translators of the King James Version.

Updated, and even vernacular, language editions are becoming increasingly available. The Goodspeed, Moffatt, Berkeley, and Amplified Bibles are examples, while such New Testament versions as Phillips, Norlie, Williams, Weymouth, The New International Version, and others leave little to be desired in efforts to express the message in contemporary terms. Many find *The Living Bible* to be a particularly helpful paraphrase.

Confused by all these translations, revisions, and versions? No need to be. Just keep one fact in the front of your mind always: this happens to be God's Word, not man's word. God will honor the conveyor that is faithful to the truth of his message. He's already promised that centuries ago. Those who fail to transmit the Word according to his original purpose won't make a dent.

For example, he has honored the King James Version to the degree that it is still performing its work more effectively than all subsequent variations of the Bible put together. What else produced in the seventeenth century is in such evidence today? You may wish to consult any or all of the versions available—I find this most helpful and stimulating in particular phases of textual study. But overall, I seldom find a substantial improvement over the King James language.

Let's take just one example. Where the King James Version reads "All things work together for good to them that love God" (Rom. 8:29), the variant reading in the Revised Standard Version is "In everything God works for good with those who love him." There may be a slight difference in wording that the Bible scholar finds interesting to pore over, but the meaning to me is unchanged. No matter how many ways it's expressed, it tells me that if I'm on God's side, I've got it made.

The Unstoppable Message

The point I am making is this: translations and revisions can't divert God's message. The Holy Spirit who authored the Bible is certainly able to project the two-edged blade of truth right through to your consciousness and to mine. Now, you couldn't make such a statement about any other book. Translations have been known to introduce down-right comical errors into human literature, and those errors have thrived.

Let's take another example, this one also written in the seventeenth century not long after the King James Version appeared. You know about Cinderella and her glass slipper, don't you? Of course, just about everybody does—but just about everybody is wrong! Charles Perrault, who put the famous fairy tale down in French, gave Cinderella a *"pantoufle en vair,"* which according to the French dictionaries (look it up) means "fur slipper." But a translator rendering the delightful story into English inadvertantly read it as *"pantoufle en verre,"* which would have truly been a glass slipper.

Of course, discrepancies in fairy tales make no difference to anybody. But if the Bible contains the words of life, it would have to be immune to the error that plagues human communication. God tolerates nothing less than unadulterated truth. You can depend on what he says.

The assertion that you have to believe the Bible "from cover to cover" is usually made with the proper motive, but it is obviously an overstatement. The editorial aids and study helps which appear in practically all editions are clearly not a part of the Scriptures. For example, the first complete Bibles were printed with the text solid and unbroken. In 1227, readability was greatly improved in England by the introduction of chapter divisions, and, in France, by the separation and numbering of verses by Robert Stephens in the year 1546.

The chronological tables which you find in the back of your Bible, and which can be most useful, were formulated in 1677 by a churchman named James Ussher. You may find two or three comparative time tables as the dates were revised by later authorities, and these are not in exact agreement with each other. Such chronologies are, of course, approximations which do not have to be relied on as absolutely correct.

The italicized words which are sprinkled throughout the King James Version were put there to indicate that they do not appear in the original manuscripts but were added to make the interpretation clear and understandable. This is an unavoidable problem for all translators.

In similar fashion, scholars and editors have appended marginal notes, maps, cross references, red letters to identify the words spoken by Jesus, brief concordances, dictionaries, and any number of such guides to facilitate a more thorough study of the Bible.

Any way you look at it, the Bible is a multilingual phenomenon. Where language differences have served to bottle up the holy book of the Muslim religion (the Koran appears in not more than a half-dozen tongues besides Arabic), they have been shaped into almost 1,500 pipelines to transport God's message from the same part of the world to all parts of the globe.

The world's most-handled, most-debated, most-translatable volume has thus established itself in every type of societal culture as a book for all humanity. On the one hand, an oppressor of people like Napoleon Bonaparte, to whom force was a way of life, concludes rather plaintively: "The Bible is no mere book, but a living creature, with a power that conquers all that oppose it." On the other, an enlightener of people like Immanuel Kant, exults: "The existence of the Bible, as a book for the people, is the greatest benefit which the human race has ever experienced. Every attempt to belittle it is a crime against humanity."

And in between, the ordinary people of the world generation after generation, find in this Book of books answers to life itself. It takes so little faith to lay aside all doubts and join the human race.

6.
THE LIBRARY IN YOUR HANDS

The Bible is God's letter to his children. If it doesn't make sense to you, it's because you've been reading someone else's mail.

Before you are sold on a product, you have to believe in it. And you're not likely to believe in a product until you know something about it. If the Bible is truly "the engrafted word which is able to save your souls," as it claims to be, then your knowledge of its message book by book should be as complete as you can make it through persistent reading and study.

To get acquainted with the *biblia*—all sixty-six books—takes only a few minutes. To become thoroughly knowledgeable can be the adventure of a lifetime devoted to exploring the inexhaustible riches of this spiritual treasure-house. Unlike other books, the Bible contains mysteries which may not be revealed to one generation but which become urgently clear and meaningful to a later generation. Similarly, this is a book which may speak to you intimately in a way it addresses no other person, and, thus, reveal to you a private plan for living which provides you with the fulfillment you have been seeking.

Let's take a quick inventory of this compact library just to familiarize ourselves with the nature of its contents. The

easiest division to follow is this: consider four sections of
Old Testament books comprising (1) the law, (2) the histories, (3) the poetical works, and (4) the prophecies; and
four sections of New Testament books under the classifica-
tions of (1) the Gospels, (2) the acts of the apostles,
(3) the letters, and (4) the final prophecy, or apocalypse.

Old Testament

A. The Law

1. GENESIS. The book of "beginnings"—the beginning of the universe, the beginning of the
   human race, the beginning of the family, the
   beginning of sin, the beginning of redemption,
   the beginning of institutions, the beginning of
   civilization, the beginning of a "chosen race."

2. EXODUS. "The way out." Literally, the exit
   of the nation of Israel from bondage in Egypt.
   The institution of the Passover, the crossing of
   the Red Sea, the recording of the Commandments, the building of the tabernacle.

3. LEVITICUS. A book for the Levites, the tribe
   appointed to conduct the worship of Jehovah.
   Detailed regulations for observing the five ceremonial offerings and the eight national feast
   days.

4. NUMBERS. So named because of the census
   of approximately three million Israelites, but

devoted to tracing the trials and failures of the people as they wandered back and forth across the Arabian wilderness during forty austere years of preparation for serving God.

5. DEUTERONOMY. "The second giving of the law." A series of orations delivered by the aged leader, Moses, covering forty years of reminiscences but representing only two months of actual time. Quoted more often by Jesus than any other Old Testament book.

B. The Histories

6. JOSHUA. Adventure-filled narrative of the military conquest of the Promised Land of Canaan, from the first successful campaign at Jericho to the final division of the territory among the twelve tribes of Israel.

7. JUDGES. Another exciting account of national history, covering the first 350 years in the new homeland, marked by alternating periods of anarchy and reformations under a succession of fifteen tribal administrators known as judges.

8. RUTH. A delightful story set in the time of the judges, which not only supplies additional historical background but establishes the documentation of the messianic line, into which Jesus would be born 1,000 years later.

9-10. FIRST and SECOND SAMUEL. Beginning of the records of the kings of Israel and Judah. David's heroic struggle in his rise to the throne and his statesmanship that brought Israel to the pinnacle of power among the civilized nations of the world.

11-12. FIRST and SECOND KINGS. The most glorious period of the chosen nation under the splendor of Solomon's reign, and the violent civil war that permanently divided the kingdom. Furnishes biographies of the nineteen kings of Israel and the nineteen kings and one queen of Judah.

13-14. FIRST and SECOND CHRONICLES. Called in the Greek version of the Old Testament *papaleipomena* or "things omitted" from the earlier king books. Supplementary documentation with much original material.

15-16. EZRA and NEHEMIAH. Combined into a single book in the Hebrew canon. Extremely valuable records covering the exile in Babylon and restoration of the nation of Israel prior to the coming of Christ.

17. ESTHER. One of the greatest short stories ever written, affording invaluable insight regarding the life and customs of ancient Persia. Forms a fascinating link with secular history.

C. The Poetical Works

18. JOB. Considered by some (Hugo, Tennyson, Carlyle)to be the finest poem produced in early or modern times. Possibly as old as the books of Moses, it is a two-act drama in verse, dealing with mankind's knottiest problems, such as self-determination, suffering, divine justice.

19. PSALMS. Made up of 150 hymns of praise, some written to be sung antiphonally in the Temple worship. Authors include David, Solomon, Asaph, Jeduthun, the sons of Korah, and about fifty anonymous writers.

20. PROVERBS. Wisdom literature in didactic poetry form, based not on rhyming verses but on paralleled concepts. Ageless recipes for coping with the challenges of daily living.

21. ECCLESIASTES. An almost shocking mirror of human philosophy with its inevitable conclusion that "all is vanity." Convincing treatise on the futility of a life apart from God, written by a wise man out of fellowship with his Lord.

22. THE SONG OF SOLOMON. A pure love idyll in the richest Oriental imagery to be found in the Old Testament. Requires more spiritual depth to be fully appreciated than perhaps any other book of the Bible.

D. The Prophecies

23. ISAIAH. One of the most majestic pieces of writing in existence, pleading with the kingdom of Judah to trust God for deliverance from the expanding Assyrian Empire, and foretelling in relentless detail the advent, the life, and the atoning death of the Messiah.

24. JEREMIAH. Warnings to Judah of the approaching destruction and captivity at the hands of Babylon, in a style that is fragmentary but sublimely sensitive, with glimpses of the messianic hope amid predictions of doom.

25. THE LAMENTATIONS. Written by the "weeping prophet," Jeremiah, a series of five elegiac poems passionately deploring the desolation of Jerusalem during the captivity in faraway Babylon. Grouped with the prophecies in our Bible, but with the poetical works in the Hebrew canon.

26. EZEKIEL. A highly symbolic work in the apocalyptic style of John's Revelation, filled with visions centering around the siege, the fall, and the restoration of Jerusalem. Fascinating predictions of the eternal glory to be ushered in by the kingdom of Christ.

27. DANIEL. Produced, like Ezekiel, during the exile of the Jews in Babylon and recorded partly

in Chaldee and partly in Hebrew. Without question one of the most interesting of all the prophetical studies, both in relation to subsequent world history and to events yet in our own future.

28. HOSEA. The first of the "minor prophets"—minor in relation to the much longer books preceding them, but not of minor importance—addressed to the doomed kingdom of Israel and filled with tender testimony of God's love for his people.

29. JOEL. An earnest message for ancient Judah and for contemporary society calling for repentance and spiritual revival. Remarkable for its revelation of the special office of the Holy Spirit in the plan of redemption.

30. AMOS. A thundering denunciation of the godless nations of the world and perhaps the most eloquent plea for social justice and basic righteousness ever written.

31. OBADIAH. Shortest book in the Bible with a profound analysis of the struggle between the spiritual and the physical natures of man as reflected in the histories of the descendants of Jacob and Esau, and as related to God's promises.

32. JONAH. Much-loved and much-hated story of

Jonah and the great fish, discredited by skeptics but exalted forever by Jesus Christ in these unequivocal words: "An evil and adulterous generation seeketh after a sign; and there shall no sign be given to it, but the sign of the prophet Jonas. For as Jonas was three days and three nights in the whale's belly; so shall the Son of man be three days and three nights in the heart of the earth. The men of Nineveh shall rise in judgment with this generation, and shall condemn it: because they repented at the preaching of Jonas; and behold, a greater than Jonas is here" (Matt. 12:39-41).

33. MICAH. The stirring invitation of a country preacher urging both the oppressors and the oppressed in a troubled society to seek out true religion by doing justly, loving mercy, and walking humbly with their God.

34. NAHUM. A sequel to Jonah, descriptive of the utter doom for the city which had temporarily heeded the earlier prophet's warning—Nineveh. Astonishing correlation to the later historical accounts of the fall of the proud Assyrian capital to the armies of the Medes and Babylonians.

35. HABAKKUK. A short series of philosophical "complaints" and answers reminiscent of the style of the book of Job, expressing supreme confidence in the face of disaster and providing Martin Luther with his theme for the Protestant

Reformation, "the just shall live by faith."

36. ZEPHANIAH. A book of recrimination and rejoicing, denouncing the sins of an idolatrous and corrupt society and thrilling to the promised coming of a "pure language" to this earth—obviously a reference to the gospel of Jesus about six hundred years later.

37. HAGGAI. First of a trio of post-exilic prophecies and principally an exhortation to the pitiful remnant of 50,000 Jews to take heart and rebuild the flattened temple of Solomon on a solid foundation of faith in the promises of God.

38. ZECHARIAH. Brilliantly written prophecy of the approaching days of Christ on earth, presented in an intriguing series of visions and culminating with a picture of the glories of an everlasting kingdom.

39. MALACHI. The bridge between the Old and the New Testaments, summing up the destiny of a rebellious people with the final word, *curse,* and foretelling by its very title (Malachi: "messenger of the Lord") the coming of God's next prophet, John the Baptist, to "prepare the way of the Lord."

New Testament

A. The Gospels (literally, "the good news")

1. MATTHEW. Presents Christ as *king,* tracing his ancestry from the first Hebrew, Abraham, through the regal line of David and the kings of Judah; therefore, 'more direct references to the Jewish canon than the other three Gospels combined.

2. MARK. Written from the Roman point of view rather than the Hebrew, emphasizing the action, the power, the miraculous works of Jesus, with hardly a mention of Old Testament background or genealogy.

3. LUKE. The record of a Greek physician interested in the human and cultural aspects of the biography of Christ and, thus, tracing his line back through his human mother all the way to the first man, Adam; the most detailed account of the conception and the birth, as would be expected of a doctor-author; and the only Gospel to give a picture of the boyhood of Jesus.

4. JOHN. Pictures Christ not as king, activist, or man—but as deity; a theological, rather than a synoptic treatment which soars above the other three Gospels in its inspired testimony of the love of God as revealed in the Spirit-filled life and the atoning death of Jesus Christ as the Third Person of the Trinity.

B. The Acts of the Apostles

5. ACTS. Like Malachi, a pivot book—looking

back on the Four Gospels and fulfilling their predictions about the empowering of the church by the Holy Spirit, about organized mass persecution, about the beginning of worldwide evangelism—and looking ahead to the epistolary writings which comprise the remainder of the New Testament; the earliest (and still the best) volume of church history.

C. The Letters

6. ROMANS. One of the apostle Paul's thirteen epistles, this one written from Corinth to the Christians in Rome; an expounding of the total plan of salvation by faith, the finest example of Paul's method of "disputation," and—in the opinion of Samuel Taylor Coleridge—"the most profound work in existence."

7. FIRST CORINTHIANS. One of the most revealing insights into the problems of church affairs, as Paul gives detailed instructions to former pagans who had been converted by his ministry in Corinth.

8. SECOND CORINTHIANS. Produced a short time after the first letter and overflowing with Paul's marvelous witness of his own sufferings and trials and "unspeakable joy" as an undaunted minister of the gospel.

9. GALATIANS. A fascinating defense of the lib-

erty of the Christian under grace as opposed to the legalistic demands of "Judaizers" who would impose the restrictions of the ceremonial law on new Gentile converts; addressed to the fickle descendants of the Gauls (Galatians) in Asia Minor, where Paul established most of his churches.

10. EPHESIANS. A powerful discourse written in prison at Rome and sent to the great church at Ephesus, stressing the unity of the churches as the body of Christ and outlining the daily walk and the lifelong warfare demanded of true believers.

11. PHILIPPIANS. Perhaps the most inspirational of Paul's letters, despite the fact that he was in chains as he composed it, urging the church he had founded at Philippi—the first Christian church in all Europe—to rejoice always in their salvation regardless of this world's hostility.

12. COLOSSIANS. An excellent reminder to all Christians that it is Christ—not theology, not religion, not philosophy, not the church—Christ alone who provides redemption from sin; prompted by reports of heresies in the Gentile church at Colosse.

13-14. FIRST and SECOND THESSALONIANS. The most explicit discussion of the second coming in the New Testament, replying to questions raised by the Christians at the Greek port of Thessalonica.

15. FIRST TIMOTHY. An intimate, fatherly letter to the young pastor who had earlier been converted by the preaching of Paul at Lystra in Asia Minor, advising him on the heroic role Timothy must fill as a minister in one of the pioneer churches.

16. SECOND TIMOTHY. Paul's farewell to his "son in the faith" written while facing execution at the hands of Nero in Rome; one of the most triumphant statements on record of a life wholly committed to Christ.

17. TITUS. The third so-called "pastoral epistle," designed to offer Titus the same sort of godly instruction for his difficult ministry in Crete that Paul had provided to Timothy in Ephesus.

18. PHILEMON. A revealing personal letter of only one short chapter to a Christian convert in Colosse, in which Paul asks Philemon to receive a runaway slave, Onesimus, back into his home on a completely new basis as a fellow Christian.

19. HEBREWS. Written in the style of Paul (although authorship is undetermined) to the Jewish Christians in Jerusalem; a masterpiece of argumentation, drawing heavily from Old Testament teachings to demonstrate the superiority

of Christ over prophets, priests, Mosaic law, Levitical ceremony, and the angels of heaven as the Savior of the world.

20. JAMES. A "wisdom book" after the pattern of Proverbs and Ecclesiastes concerned not so much with a saving faith as with a practical faith with its resulting good works, which should be the identifying evidence of every Christian life.

21. FIRST PETER. A vigorous and direct appeal to the churches in the mission field to face without fear the worsening conditions of Roman persecution; rugged and simple, yet sublime in its message of hope and consolation.

22. SECOND PETER. A warning to the churches to be on guard against apostasy within and fearful threats from without, Peter's eloquence and bravery giving startling evidence of the transformation that has taken place within the man who had previously three times denied his Lord.

23. FIRST JOHN. One of the most earnest, most persuasive, and most impassioned books of the entire Bible in its effort to reveal the urgency of believing and knowing and experiencing Jesus Christ as truth and God as love.

24. SECOND JOHN. A very short epistle on testing the validity of the truth of the gospel to expose

false teachers; only book addressed to an "elect lady."

25. THIRD JOHN. A personal note to a wealthy church patron named Gaius on John's favorite subject of truth, branding one Diotrephes as one of the false teachers to be shunned.

26. JUDE. The last of the New Testament letters, written by Jude, the brother of Jesus, as an outspoken condemnation of the heretics who practice their opposition to the cause of Christ within the framework of his church.

D. The Final Prophecy

27. REVELATION. One of the Bible's most-studied books, the climax of scriptural communication; linked with the Old Testament prophecies of Ezekiel and Daniel in its apocalyptic language, packed with referents to history, both secular and ecclesiastical, which are clearly decipherable although clothed in mysterious symbolism; a glorious revealing of the splendors of heaven and the frightful events which will close out the age.

There you have it, a veritable bookmobile containing the most widely traveled, most universally known library in existence. Sixty-six books covering about 1600 years certainly offer the reader a diversity of information he is not likely to find anywhere else bound in a single volume.

And yet, through that exciting process which the serious student of the Bible comes to recognize as progressive revelation, God unfolds to us a harmonious, unified account of his plan of redemption. It flows through every book from Genesis to Revelation like a clear crystal stream, revealing a unity of purpose and design and direction that is truly phenomenal.

While all of its parts are equally inspired, it does not follow that every book is as important as every other book, any more than all the parts of our body could be said to be of parallel importance. The book of Hebrews may have more to say than the book of Lamentations, and the tiny prophecy of Habakkuk certainly is overshadowed by the Psalms or by the Gospel of Matthew as far as sheer content is concerned. But the Bible is a whole, and each book makes its essential contribution to the complete oneness of the total work.

You may read at random from this great Book and reap benefits, for "all scripture is given by inspiration of God, and is profitable for doctrine, for reproof, for correction, for instruction in righteousness" (2 Tim. 3:16). But to comprehend fully the spiritual consistency of this matchless compendium is a challenge to workman-like studiousness and devotion to the search for truth.

Can you doubt it?

7.
SCIENCE
VERSUS
SCRIPTURE:
NO CONTEST

*Now the evolutionists have the monkey worrying
about whether he is his brother's keeper or his
keeper's brother.*

For many of us, our introduction to the marvels of the
world of scientific knowledge was accompanied by a chill-
ing exposure to the first real, deep-down doubts we ever
experienced. Science seemed to tell us so confidently of
things the Bible apparently was unaware of, and much
of what we had accepted as scriptural truth suddenly appeared to be lacking in the neatly catalogued clinical evidence that can be so convincing.

But back off and take a fresh look. There's no conflict
at all between science and the Bible or between science
and religion. There may be some conflict somewhere, but
it's not here.

Science and the Bible are partners. They share the common purpose of disclosing and establishing truth. Both
strive to reduce complicated concepts to simplest expressions: "$E = mc^2$" and "God is love" are simplifications.
So are "A straight line is the shortest distance between
two points," and "Except a man be born again, he cannot
see the kingdom of God" (John 3:3).

Don't imagine a conflict where none exists. These sup-

posed antagonists emanate from the same source. They
have the same Author.

Science is described as "accumulated knowledge sys-
tematized and formulated with reference to the discovery
of general truths or the operation of general laws." Whose
truths? Whose laws? One of the fathers of science, Aristotle,
observed early in the game that "the structure of the universe is the work of a Great Intelligence. Law reigns everywhere."

Far more intimately acquainted with that Great Intelligence was the psalmist, who doesn't equivocate in his
address to the God of the Bible: "Thy law is the truth"
(Ps. 119:142). Basing his observations on experience and
on documentation, David is thoroughly scientific in identifying the Bible as the fountain of knowledge: "I have
more understanding than all my teachers: for thy testimonies are my meditation. I understand more than the
ancients, because I keep thy precepts" (Ps. 119:99-100).

The affinity between science and God's Word is real.
Are you aware that a practical scientist mentioned by name
in the Bible was elevated and blessed above all the people
of his time? If you will read in the first chapter of the
book of Daniel, you will discover that the great monarch
Nebuchadnezzar, who ruled the Babylonian empire, ordered his commissioner of education to "bring certain of
the children of Israel . . . skilful in all wisdom, and cunning in knowledge, and understanding science, and such
as had ability in them to stand in the king's palace, and
whom they might teach the learning and the tongue of
the Chaldeans" (Dan. 1:3-4).

Because he was mentally sharp—"skilful in all wisdom,
and cunning in knowledge, and understanding science"—

and because he used that gift to magnify the name of God and to glorify his authority among the heathen with such success that he finally converted the king himself, this man Daniel stands today as one of the most illustrious figures in the Old Testament.

Was he torn by any conflict between his science and his religion? Was the brilliance of his mind involved in a showdown battle with the purity of his heart? Did his career of knowledge militate against his dedication to worship? If you've read the book, you know the answers. The young scientist himself tells you where his information comes from: "I will shew thee that which is noted in the scripture of truth" (Dan. 10:21).

The primal power of the universe is a mystery, whether seen through the eyes of religion or the eyes of science. It is behind all discernible energy—that which we can follow into motion and matter—and behind all energy which we haven't begun to understand. Scientific theory seeks to explain and to define, as far as its methodology will allow, this ultimate authority as physical truth. The Bible seeks to reveal this primal power as *spiritual* truth, the same Author-ity.

The findings of science and the teachings of Scripture-based religion bring us to a recognition of the same ultimate authority or power source. Both point to the one true God.

If there is no disharmony, then why the endless arguments that some indulge in, pitting science against religion, or seeing science as disproving the Bible? It's because of an adulterating ingredient which we haven't brought into the mix yet. So far, we have talked about truth, and that automatically excludes conflict. Truth is truth, no matter

how we approach it.
Let's chart it this way:

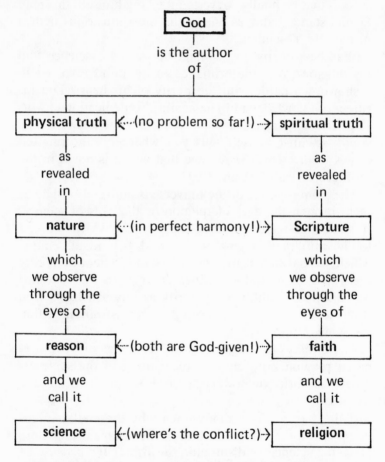

So let's introduce at this point the catalyst which is responsible for whatever controversy rages. Let's isolate it and give it its proper identification. All of the arguments that have ever been launched under the banners of the science *versus* religion–war have been generated from one and the same source: *error.*

Alternative to Truth

When error is part of the picture, we are no longer talking about science and religion. We have begun to deal with a new commodity—either with pseudoscience or with pseudoreligion, or perhaps with both. Most assuredly there is, and always must be, deadly opposition between pseudoscience and the Bible, and between pseudoreligion and science. Conflict here is inevitable and interminable simply because of the nature of truth and error.

Science can easily and quickly pick out the fatal flaws of false religion, or of Scripture falsely interpreted. The truth of the Bible instantly exposes and indicts the erroneous conclusions of a pseudoscience, no matter how intriguing or appealing the evidence may be made to appear.

You're not sure about this? Let's quote directly from the Bible and from some of the most respected men of science. It won't be necessary to make more than one reference to the inspired text, and we find one in Paul's first letter to the young preacher, Timothy.

The alert mind of the veteran evangelist, which had been exposed to the pseudoscience of the Athenian intellectuals, shows the lucid discrimination that would serve many modern "thinkers" well. He warns Timothy about something that every young man has to be shown: "O Timothy, keep that which is committed to thy trust, avoiding profane and vain babblings, and oppositions of science . . ."—but Paul doesn't stop there—" . . . falsely so called; which some professing have erred concerning the faith" (1 Tim.

6:20-21).

Did you get it? The Scripture didn't say "the oppositions of science," but "the oppositions of science falsely so called." You might prefer the Norlie translation of the New Testament passage, which reads, "the oppositions of pseudo-science."

Paul could just as easily have warned against "religion falsely so called." That was the thing that ruined the kingdom of Israel. That's what Jesus so relentlessly upbraided the Pharisees for. And that's what ruins countless lives today—far more than pseudoscience does.

Where the layman may have great difficulty in knowing the difference between true science and false science, there is one sure test. Take any knowledgeable scientist to whom God has given the mental capacity, the time, and the resources to make intelligent decisions. When and if he comes to the point where he attempts to minimize the ultimate authority (to leave God out), you can be sure there is something wrong with him somewhere. At that point, he begins to think like a pseudoscientist.

We were going to quote from a few of the scientists themselves. In an effort to bring representative viewpoints together, let's range from some of the earlier pioneers to contemporary experts:

> *Sir William Herschel.* "All human discoveries seem to be made only for the purpose of confirming more and more strongly the truths contained in the Holy Scriptures."

> *Isaac Newton.* "There are more marks of authority in the Bible than in any profane history."

J. H. Pratt. "The book of nature and the Word of God emanate from the same infallible Author, and therefore can not be at variance. But man is a fallible interpreter, and by mistaking one or both of the Divine Records, he forces them often into unnatural conflict."

James Dwight Dana. "I, an old man who has known only science all his life long, say to you, that there is nothing truer in all the universe than the scientific statements contained in the Word of God."

Dr. George Wald, a current winner of the Nobel Prize in the field of science. "I am convinced that the only way to prevent the total chaos that we are headed for, and probably within the next ten years, is to return to God and the Bible."

Dr. Wernher Von Braun, who masterminded the V-2 rocket of Germany in World War II and the space program of the United States for two decades, said in a speech at Taylor University. "The idea of an orderly universe is inconceivable without God—the grandeur of the cosmos confirms the certainty of a creation. One can't be exposed to the law and order of the universe without becoming aware of a divine intent."

A contemporary news article from United Press International: "For a long time, some people have expected and others have feared that modern science eventually would discredit the basic postulates of religion.

"But just the opposite is actually happening. Instead

of undermining belief in God, science is finding more and more evidence of 'the existence of a reality beyond the natural order' " so says Dr. William G. Pollard . . . a nuclear physicist, a pioneer in atomic research, and director of the Associated Universities of Oak Ridge, Tennessee.

"Pollard has never found it necessary to compartmentalize his mind in order to combine these two roles. On the contrary, he says, the knowledge gained from daily scientific research has deepened his religious convictions, while the insights of religion have made him better able to comprehend the workings of the natural universe.

"Therefore, he says, the 'most important discovery that anyone can make today' is the discovery of the reality of God."

These men have taken their battle stations. And like them—whether you realize it or not—you're also right up on the firing line. The battle between truth and error, just like wars between the nations, has to be fought by individuals. It's a battle for your mind, and where pseudoreligion might not trouble you to the extent it has bothered others, watch out for pseudoscience! In this sophisticated age, particularly, it has proved itself to be a persuasive master of deceit.

Let's get specific. For about three generations now, we have seen the undeniable fascination which the theory of biological evolution has had over inquisitive minds when they reach the upper high school and college levels. I call it the "theory" advisedly, because to this date its entitlement to the label of "science" remains unearned. Don't take my word for it, but call on someone whose credentials you will recognize—Albert Einstein. He said: "I have found that Darwin's, Haeckel's, and Huxley's theories are now completely antiquated."

I will venture beyond this authoritative detraction of the evolutionary theory and suggest that it be plainly labeled as a pseudoscience. I am impressed by Professor Frank Marsh's statement that "if evolutionists had not wasted a generation of hard work trying to pick up a trail which never existed, biology would be at least a generation farther along in the discovery of laws and processes which do exist." On what grounds can we brand it as a pseudoscience? Simply on those previously stated: any theorist who attempts to minimize God (and thus to glorify man) has missed the truth somewhere and can not be completely trusted. Conversely, it is to be expected that such a person will be suspicious of the teachings of the Bible.

Let's be fair now and give the early advocates of organic evolution equal time:

> *Charles Darwin.* "I am aware that the assumed instinctive belief in God has been used by many persons as an argument for his existence. But this is a rash argument."

> *Ernst Heinrich Haeckel.* "The world system is pantheism. Atheism is only another expression for it, emphasizing its negative aspect, the nonexistence of any supernatural deity."

> *Thomas Henry Huxley.* "The exact nature of the

teachings and the convictions of Jesus is extremely uncertain. . . . The cosmic process has no sort of relation to moral ends."

H. G. Wells. "If man evolved . . . then the entire historic fabric of Christianity . . . the story of the first sin and reason for an atonement—collapses like a house of cards."

Sir Arthur Keith. "We believe it (evolution) because the only alternative is special creation; and that is unthinkable."

Julian Huxley (grandson of Thomas Henry). "Evolution, if consistently accepted, makes it impossible to believe the Bible."

Other, and more recent, devotees could be quoted, but these are sufficient to establish the fact that the idea of evolution is basically opposed to trust in God and in his Word.

The plain facts are that the original theory has long since run its course so far as the top-drawer experts are concerned. But successive generations of laymen and scientologists still find the hypothesis so seductive and exciting that they continue to latch on to it as some new gospel. And why shouldn't they? They are generously aided and abetted by well-intentioned teachers, movie producers, newspaper reporters, and even encyclopedias and museums, many of whom present the whole business as though it were fact rather than theory. The world takes excellent care of its own.

I don't presume to diminish the reputation of dedicated naturalists like Lamarck and Darwin and others who spent a lifetime gathering data from all parts of the globe, and I confess to the thrill of excitement with which I first pored through *The Origin of the Species* and *The Descent of Man* as a college student, as though I were making some new discovery. And you and I are aware that many books have been put together on the subject in far more painstaking and sophisticated terms than are used in this brief chapter. But the core of the assumption and its fatal weaknesses can be bared completely in the space of a few paragraphs.

What the theory of evolution asks you to believe is that all life forms have developed from preexisting types of a lower, unidentifiable order; that man, therefore, through millions of years has evolved from some previous animal modification; that whatever human qualities he possesses have developed as the creature progressed up the scale of life forms all the way from a one-cell marine organism to today's highly complex mechanism known as Homo sapiens.

The Way Things Look

On what does the evolutionist base this assumption? On just one thing: appearances. Yes, man can be considered a member of the "animal kingdom" insofar as he obviously doesn't appear to be a mineral or a vegetable. Yes, he can be listed in what the biologist calls the phylum of chordates, since the words mean only that he is equipped with a nerve cord like many other creatures. And you can also call him a vertebrate, which means that he has a hollow backbone such as is found in a shark or a horse or a squirrel.

Still going by the appearances of things, the biological evolutionist is soon classifying right out the window. Because he finds man to be a vertebrate whose young are born alive instead of hatched from eggs, and who is hair-covered, furnished with mammary glands, and warm-blooded, he feels that he must classify man as a mammal along with most of the familiar beasts of the world. Next, he observes that by reason of his fingers, thumbs, and nails, Homo sapiens is one of a distinguished order of pawless, clawless mammals known as primates ("chief mammals"); this admits him to the company of apes, monkeys, lemurs, and tarsiers.

From here on it begins to get scary. Just three of this primate crew are given the title of "upward-looking beings" or anthropoids. Man is built with an erect posture, so he belongs. And when you look at both monkeys and apes, you have to admit that they sometimes stand up on their hind legs, too. So, from this suborder of anthropoids, it's just a teeny step to the family of hominids.

It is at this point that we pass from what might be just innocent observation of similar appearances into the fantasy sphere, for *hominid* is a coined word meaning "man-like." You have seen hundreds of drawings and three-dimensional reproductions of creatures which were half-man and half-ape. But you've never seen a hominid, because it exists only in theory. All you have seen up to this point are monkeys, apes, and men—and a few hundred conjectures built about the imaginary hominid.

Believable? I suppose that depends on who you are. Before you accept such hypotheses as facts, you should amass as much scientific knowledge as Von Braun, the recognized technological genius of the twentieth century, who dismisses the theory with a comment: "There are those who argue that the universe evolved out of a random process, but what random process could produce the brain of a man or the system of the human eye?" When a man of science is a man of faith, he doesn't become an inferior scientist—he simply becomes a superior man.

But what about the evidence? Indeed, where is the evidence? If the earth is 4.5 billion years old, its crust would surely have yielded a representative sampling by now of thousands upon thousands of well-defined specimens of hominid remains. The laws of probability would require at least that many as a basis of proof, and the theory of a "missing link" between man and animal would have been as firmly established as the tested formulas of mathematics we have come to accept.

But do you know how many bits and pieces the whole idea of human evolution has been built upon? Not enough to fill one pickup truck. For instance, there's Neanderthal man and his misshapen skull; I have seen living specimens who have much the same appearance. And Cro-Magnon man, who incidentally, was equal to any man alive today, and superior to many. His brain-to-spinal-column ratio was 33-1, exactly the same as yours and mine. Highly touted are the fragments of jawbone and skull cap which have been personalized with such names as Heidelberg Man, and Peking Man, and Java Man, and all the others, along with fancied portraits to match.

One of the most widely publicized series of discoveries has to do with skeletal portions of about 100 individuals found in Africa, beginning with Raymond Dart's find in 1924. The Australopithecines, as they are known, were hailed as some sort of "missing link" creatures which built fires, used tools, and lived in social groups. These imaginative claims have been questioned by others who have unearthed similar evidence. Dr. L. S. B. Leakey of the Coryndon Memorial Museum in Kenya, speaking to a gathering of scientists attending the Darwin Centennial in Chicago, announced that (1) no real evidence of the use of fire had ever been found, (2) the stone fragments he originally identified as tools had proved to be no tools at all, and (3) the Australopithecines were incapable of speech and therefore without the social structures that derive only from true language orientation. Whatever kind of primate the Australopithecines represent, Professor Irving Hallowell of the University of Pennsylvania concludes, "They were not human in the sense that we are human."

No one denies for a moment that this is high adventure. It's downright exciting to dream along with the theorists on what spooky types might have climbed up the rungs of the reconstructed evolutionary ladder. And it's worth investigating, of course, despite the fact that some of these reconstructed specimens turned out to be hilarious fakes—like Piltdown Man (invented by a student who fooled the experts for half a century) and Nebraska Man (his reputation was established on a single fossilized tooth, which was eventually found to belong to a long-dead pig).

But to get so infatuated with the evolutionary hypothesis that you can be sold a bill of goods about mankind progressively remodeling itself through natural selection from beast to benefactor, would be to demonstrate a capacity for credulity that even the Bible does not require. So man is evolving upward from bestiality toward perfection, is he? Let me add to our list of specimens that rare example from the twentieth century: Nazi Man, who revived the tribal art of torture, and with superb efficiency, roasted 6,000,000 of his fellow humans in his gas ovens. And, just in passing let me remind you that Perfect Man walked the earth almost 2,000 years ago—a bit ahead of his evolutionary time, wouldn't you say?

Seriously, the scientific method demands far more than the theory of biological evolution has been able to supply. Therefore, it remains a diverting kind of speculation based on the engaging similarities in life forms, past and present. Undoubtedly, there are seemingly endless variations in animal, plant, and human life, and many genetic patterns within the species. Why shouldn't there be some remarkable similarities in human and animal physical structures? God obviously followed a consistent pattern of creation. Whether you observe the submicroscopic pattern of whirling protons inside a human cell or the astronomic movements of worlds hurtling through space, you are overwhelmed by the infinite "consistency of variety" in God's universe.

I stand amazed, as well as amused, at discoveries of startling analogies between species. It does *look* as though whales and boas have remnants of hind legs, but it really doesn't *prove* they had legs. It's easy to *imagine* that man's coccyx was once elongated into a tail or that his appendix was once a second stomach or that he walked on all fours—if you want to *imagine* it. It is delightful to explore the *history* of eohippus, which apparently came in a wide variety of graduated sizes, judging from fossil evidence; but whether you wish to link the specimens together as an argument for the *evolution* of modern horse is up to you.

And from what we can now observe of the human fetus

through its successive stages of development, it truly does *appear* to have at times the characteristics of an amoeba, a fish, an amphibian, a reptile, a fowl, and a mammal. But you've got to be some special kind of dreamer to suppose this miraculous nine-month process justifies the absurd notion (known as the recapitulation theory) that all this actually is a sort of instant replay of the eon-by-eon unfolding of organic evolution. No matter what it may *resemble* at a given stage, the prenatal form is never anything less than thoroughly human from beginning to end.

I respect scholarship wherever I find it. But I lose respect for the scholar when he reaches the point in his reasoning that he decides, sadly but sagely, that he must remove the Creator from his creation—as though he really could! No matter how impressive his research, if it ultimately leads him to doubt the honesty of God's inspired Word—and the very existence of God Himself—he becomes just another deluded intellectual. He is no longer being scientific—just pseudoscientific. It was Agassiz who declared that "any man who accepts the doctrine of evolution ceases thereby to be a man of science." God and truth cannot be separated anywhere down the line. He is the author of natural as well as moral truth.

Theistic Evolution Won't Cut It

The sincere doubter will sooner or later question whether there isn't a legitimate option left open for believing in "theistic evolution." Couldn't God have "permitted" the evolutionary process as part of his sovereign plan? Well, as a matter of sheer argument, of course he could have if he had willed to. But as a matter of record, he reveals to us that he didn't do it that way because it would have been inconsistent with his very nature. He tells us that he made man at the top of the ladder, as a perfect being in his own image, and that man has fallen to the level of bestiality because he allowed sin to come into his life.

The Bible is the story of man's need for a redeemer from this sinful state. Man evolving from lower to higher stages of physical and moral development would need no redemption, because the accidents of nature are somehow accomplishing the job on their own.

Theistic evolution is a myth which reverses God's whole revelation of his program of redemption. If you accept it, you must then attempt to mythologize God's Word, as many have tried to do.

We haven't suggested yet that the man of faith is forced to reject a single fact disclosed by science—not one. But he must have the wisdom to discriminate between facts and theories predicated on those facts. Poor Thomas Henry Huxley was the prime promoter of Darwin's theory, but he didn't believe it! His final conclusion reflects the torment of agnosticism: "Looking back through the prodigious vistas of time, I find no record of the beginning of life, and therefore I am devoid of any means of forming a conclusion as to the conditions of its appearance. . . . Belief, in the scientific sense of the word, is a serious matter and requires strong foundations. To say, therefore, in the admitted absence of evidence, that I have any belief as to the mode in which life forms have originated, would be using the words in the wrong sense."

No belief! The tragic utterance of those who walk by sight instead of by faith. What a blessed contrast of assurance and conviction the Bible truth proclaims: "What is man, that thou art mindful of him? and the son of man, that thou visitest him? For thou hast made him a little lower than the angels [it doesn't say a little higher than the animals], and hast crowned him with glory and honor. Thou hast made him to have dominion over the works of thy hands; thou hast put all things under his feet" (Ps. 8:4-6).

There's God's answer to man's theory. *Beware of counterfeits:* "As we have borne the image of the earthy [that's what fools the evolutionist], we shall also bear the image of the heavenly" (1 Cor. 15:49). Don't be misled by appearances: "Things which are seen were not made of things which do appear" (Heb. 11:3).

In sum, we are to resist the temptation to walk by sight. Then we will be able to shift our priority to God's elemental commandment to walk by faith. I believe this is the directive followed by an increasing majority of men of science, anyway. The American Scientific Affiliation has published this statement of faith: "The Holy Scriptures are the inspired Word of God, the only unerring guide of faith and conduct. Jesus Christ is the Son of God and through his atonement is the one and only Mediator between God and man."

The real issue, you see, is not your decision about *what* to believe—it's your decision about *whether* to believe. If your head can't consider a theory of biological evolution without your heart embracing a religion of biological determinism, wouldn't it be more intelligent to defer the risk altogether? Is the hypothesis worth sacrificing everything for? If you gain the whole evolutionary world and lose your own soul, where's your profit?

The Hard Facts

Do you have any difficulty in reconciling the geologic

ages, as attested by the record of the rocks, with the scriptural version of six days of creation? Then you have no problem at all unless the language bothers you. The term *day* can be made to represent twenty-four hours, or it can stand for a geologic age; "the day of the Lord" is a common biblical expression signifying the final dispensation or era.

There is all the room you need between Genesis 1:1 and 1:2 for billions of years of development. Contemporary scholars are seeing three phases of creation packed into those two short verses—a perfect earth (generation), a "void" earth marred by satanic influence (degeneration), and a remade earth salvaged from the havoc wrought by eons of darkness and freezing (regeneration). It's a fascinating approach, and entirely consistent with the Bible's explanation of God's procedure in human redemption: made, marred, remade.

No one doubts that the rocks are telling the truth about the age of the earth, which geologists place as something like 4.5 billion years. However, I wouldn't rule out the possibility of God's having created the universe in six 24-hour days, *if that happened to be the way he chose to do it.* But science and the Bible seem to be in perfect harmony in their report of progressive creation, as the following breakdown indicates:

Geology calls it	*Bible calls it*
AZOIC PERIOD Means "no life." Creation processes still going on. About 4.5 billion years ago.	FIRST DAY No life created yet. God made light (Gen. 1:3) which precedes life forms.

ARCHEOZOIC PERIOD

Means "age before life." Earth's crust cooling in atmosphere and intermittently covered by water. About 2.1 billion years ago.

PROTEROZOIC PERIOD

Means "primitive life." Almost no traces of organisms from this period, except for a few sponges and limy sea plants. About 1 billion years ago.

PALEOZOIC PERIOD

Means "ancient life." Tides still cover the continents, but apparently under lunar influence now. Few fossil remains of sea scorpions and shell fish. About 500 million years ago.

MESOZOIC PERIOD

Means "middle life." Bathed in full sunlight, life begins to teem in global swamplands where seas are retreating. Fish, reptiles (including dinosaurs), and birds leave abundant fossil evidence in earth's crust. About 200 million years ago.

CENOZOIC PERIOD

Means "recent life." Land

SECOND DAY

Still no life. God created a firmament with waters above and below (Gen. 1:6) atmosphere so thick it hid the sun and moon, and surface waters.

THIRD DAY

Some dry land appearing in midst of global seas. God created grass, herbs, and earliest plant life (Gen. 1:9-12).

FOURTH DAY

Atmospheric envelope thinning out so that sun and moon become visible. God stabilized the orbits of the "two great lights" and of the earth itself, winding up the clock of the solar system, and thus creating the tides to which life on earth adjusted (Gen. 1:14-18).

FIFTH DAY

"And God said, Let the waters bring forth abundantly the moving creature that hath life, and fowl that may fly above the earth in the open firmament of heaven. And God created great whales, and every living creature that moveth" (Gen. 1:20-21).

SIXTH DAY

God made the "beast of the

mammals appear on the scene, then man shows up and begins hunting and domesticating animals, leaving artifacts of weapons and tools as evidence. About 60 million years ago for mammals, perhaps no more than 10,000 years ago for man.

earth" (for hunting) and "cattle after their kind" (for domesticating), insect life, and myriad forms of "creeping things." Then "God created man in his own image, in the image of God created he him; male and female created he them " (Gen. 1:27).

The parallelism is remarkable, isn't it? Bible chronologers estimate the creation of man to be about 6,000 years ago (the Bible itself is silent on the issue), as compared with geology's guess of something past 10,000 years. I believe we could call this extremely close tolerance in a 4.5-billion-year schedule, and science is still revising its timetables as more evidence is uncovered and as the once "reliable" carbon 14 and potassium-argon dating method of measuring the age of rocks and artifacts have come up with discrepancies exceeding one million years!

Where did the inspired writer of Genesis get his information? He had no scientist to consult with. He had to get it from the Holy Spirit, who reaffirms the same unchanging truth in the pages of the Bible today: "for the pillars [the geologist calls them rocks] of the earth are the Lord's and he hath set the world upon them" (1 Sam. 2:8).

What science is slowly discovering is that the universe and its appointed overlord, man, were created as an act of love. Astronomy's older theories of accidental creation—the "big bang" approach—are dying out. No number of explosions in a type foundry could accidentally produce a dictionary, and you could rattle seventeen metal components around in a washtub for billions of years without ever accidentally producing an electric can opener. Sir William Dawson, Canada's noted geologist, found his knowledge no barrier to understanding that "Man was created as the Hebrew literally reads."

What the Stars Tell Us

Perhaps it is in the fathomless reaches of the study of astronomy that the mind of man undergoes its most vigorous stretching. His faith tends to get lost in the vast dimensions of infinity as he contemplates earth's seeming insignificance among more than ten billion known galaxies, each of which includes uncounted billions of stars larger than his own. Man's recent achievements in space travel shrink to nothingness when he is reminded that, even if he could travel at the speed of light—eleven million miles a minute—he would need 80,000 years just to travel from one end of our familiar Milky Way galaxy to the other.

Is the God of such immensity really interested in one little grain of dust called earth? Perhaps he has other populations billions of light years away about whom he is more concerned. These are imponderables that can be answered only one way: "Through faith we understand that the worlds were framed by the word of God" (Heb. 11:3). That all-sufficient Word of God was made available to you and me to provide that which we absolutely need to know, and to enable us to trust the Creator for all the things we can't know.

But astronomy has taught us one important thing so far: nothing exactly like our earth has yet been observed anywhere in the universe. Professor Jesse L. Greenstein of the California Institute of Technology reports that the earth is "a distinct abnormality in the universe. . . . Our earth and solar system are abnormal in that they are not in the mainstream of chemical and nuclear processes in stars."

This would mean, of course, that man made of the dust of the earth is also a unique creature. That same reliable Word of God informs us that he is indeed the culmination of all God's handiwork, and that the overwhelming grandeur of the universe testifies to the tremendous value that he places on mankind.

Let me enlarge on the scriptural assessment quoted earlier: "When I consider thy heavens, the work of thy fingers, the moon and the stars, which thou hast ordained; what is man, that thou art mindful of him? and the son of man, that thou visitest him? For thou hast made him a little lower than the angels, and hast crowned him with glory and honour. Thou madest him to have dominion over the works of thy hands" (Ps. 8:3-6).

Search any direction you wish into the discoveries of science and you find astonishing harmony with the assurances of the Bible. Only in the realm of "science falsely so called" will you find the soul-disturbing, faith-shattering claims that set themselves up in arrogant opposition to the Scriptures which teach that "God is love" and that consequently, as an expression of that love, "the Lord God made the earth and the heavens."

To say that there is no conflict between true science and Scripture-based religion is not to say that there isn't a difference. Of course there is an essential difference. The scientific method is rational, impersonal, and amoral—not involved in moral considerations. The religious method is intuitive, personal, and intrinsically moral. Scientific exploration discovers God to be omniscient, omnipresent, and omnipotent; religious exploration reveals him to be not only infinite in his knowledge, presence, and power but also perfect in his righteousness, mercy, justice, and what the Bible calls "lovingkindness."

In functional terms, the difference means that science is a tool to be used to whatever limits changing conditions decree to be expedient. Religion, on the other hand, is a way of life built on faith in moral and spiritual values which are unchanging. Science, being amoral, can give us television, submarines, nuclear fission, and birth control pills without any regard for the consequences. Our use or misuse of these outputs will depend upon our attitude toward the Bible.

At its very best, then, science can make contributions to the quality of life on this earth, and nothing beyond for you or me. Religion rooted in God's Word interprets not only our present existence, but life everlasting, in the most meaningful terms. Consequently, a naive faith in the capacity of science to solve all of our problems is a sure sign of spiritual immaturity. Once you have, through faith, a firm grip on eternity, you're not going to become disoriented by the passing achievements of technology—no matter how spectacular they may become during your allotted dimension of time on earth.

Put First Things First

To state it bluntly, what man needs most of all is salvation, and science can't save. "For by grace are ye saved through faith; and that not of yourselves: it is the gift of God" (Eph. 2:8).

Keeping this basic difference in mind, then—that the Bible's purpose is spiritual redemption whereas science's is the exploration of natural phenomena—nobody could expect the Scriptures to read like a science textbook. The language would logically be elemental, understandable to all generations of people throughout the centuries and translatable into every dialect. It has no need for esoteric codes and definitions and formulas, for hypothetical and postulated language, because such terminology doesn't suit its purpose at all. It uses instead an idiom which needs no revision every few years, as other texts do, and which is universally effective in getting the message across.

For example, we all know that the sun doesn't rise and set, or that the bowels, kidneys, and heart don't really house the emotions. But the use of such commonplace expressions does no violence whatsoever to scientific data. We certainly allow our most eminent scientists the right to say "it's raining cats and dogs outside" without demanding that they deliver a lecture on the gravitational attraction of atmospheric distillation to prove that their statements can be trusted.

The truly amazing fact about these ancient writings is that even though they sometimes communicate in imprecise, prescientific language they have not yet been proved unscientific in any of their passing references to the world of nature. G. B. Hardy has delightfully summarized the unchanging scientific accuracy of the Bible, as in the following observations:

1. Once science said there were only 1056 stars in the sky. The Bible always maintained, "The stars of heaven cannot be numbered" . . . We know now, of course, that it is impossible to number the stars . . . (Jer. 33:22).

2. Scientists once maintained the earth was a flat stationary disc resting on immovable foundations . . . The Bible, however, proclaimed the earth a "sphere" which "hangeth upon nothing." It further advised man his globe "turned as clay to the seal" in motion about the sun, and that the sun itself was "in a circuit unto the end of heaven." Science today hasn't caught up entirely with this, but is fast expecting the Bible has once again evidenced prior knowledge. . . . Yes, the sun as part of its galaxy is in a huge circuit through the heavens (Isa. 40:22; Job 26:7; 38:14; Ps. 19:6).

3. "While as yet he had not made . . . the highest part of the dust of the world" . . . (Prov. 8:26) . . . what possibly could be the significance of dust in the atmosphere? We now know light reflections from particles in the atmosphere give us our colors, our blue skies, our sunsets. Consider this . . . with no dust in the "higher parts" we could have no rain, and the sky overhead would be forever black.

4. "The Lord thy God hath divided (the stars) unto all nations under the whole heaven" . . . (Deut. 4:19). Now, of course, we know due to the earth being round and because of its ordained circuit, the peoples of the northern hemisphere have their own constellations allotted in the heavens overhead and never see the constellations visible to peoples in the southern hemisphere. The

Bible said this before we knew our earth was round and in a fixed circuit.

5. "Where wast thou when I laid the foundations of the earth?" . . . (Job 38:4).

The Bible does draw our attention to the engineering feat of establishing the internal foundation of the earth.

Now when you consider the weight of the earth is established at six sextillion tons, with mountains and oceans merely floating on a thin outer crust, yet subject to three tremendous and entirely different rates of motion . . . yes, the earth's foundations are a point of some interest . . . and science now agrees . . . of some wonder.[1]

Many, many such anticipations of science in the Scriptures could be cited, from hints of gunpowder and aeronautics to foregleams of electronics and the chain reaction of splitting atoms. But one point should now be clear: the truths of the Bible, including even the most casual allusions to empirical facts, never change. They are eternal truths recorded by the Spirit of Truth, and you need never to fear that any statement of the Bible, no matter how obscure its meaning might be to us, will ever be proved obsolete or erroneous. The message of the Bible needs no revision.

Science is kept busy, on the other hand, disproving and revising its own premises. Embarrassed astronomers have erased their earlier notion that the moon generated its own light (the Bible had already advised us that "it shineth not," Job 25:5); Euclid's geometry has been rewritten, the Newtonian law of gravitation has required revision, and even the Einstein theory of relativity isn't as relative as it used to be. In fact, there simply isn't anything as relative or as relevant to you and me today as the knowledge of what God has said. To imagine that his Word is in the least jeopardized by the advances of science is to reveal not just a timidity of faith, but a lack of understanding as well.

If you seek the ability to deal with facts as they relate to life, then get down to the really challenging work of mining the priceless information hidden away in the Scriptures. The Bible can make you understand that "of his own will begat he us with the word of truth, that we should be a kind of firstfruits of his creatures. Wherefore . . . receive with meekness the engrafted word, which is able to save your souls" (Jas. 1:18,21).

Bible study involves serious digging, and it's like any other man-sized job—the more you put into it, the more you'll get out of it. How to do both is the subject of our next chapter.

---

[1] From *Countdown* by G. B. Hardy (Chicago: Moody Press, Moody Bible Institute of Chicago, 1967), p. 38. Used by permission.

8.
LEARNING TO READ

Don't expect to mine the richest lode until you have done a little prospecting for nuggets.

Do you find the Bible understandable? Does it really talk to you? Is there one consistent message that leaps out at you whether you're reading a proverb of Solomon or a section of the Levitical code or an argument from a letter addressed to a church in Asia Minor? Is God communicating to you right now in a personal way through this Word recorded centuries ago?

If not, then admit it—you haven't learned how to read the Bible. Your eyes may have traveled over every single portion from "In the beginning God created the heaven and the earth" (Gen. 1:1) right down to the final "The grace of our Lord Jesus Christ be with you all. Amen" (Rev. 22:21). But you still haven't read the Bible. All you've done is look at the words. And seeing isn't believing.

This Book is unlike any other book ever produced, in that the meaning of its contents can't be transmitted through the natural processes of discernment. This sounds strange, but it's true. This is one Book that cannot be understood unless it is spiritually discerned. That unique aspect of its nature is described very explicitly in these words:

"But as it is written, Eye hath not seen, nor ear heard, neither have entered into the heart of man, the things which God hath prepared for them that love him. But God hath revealed them unto us by his Spirit: for the Spirit searcheth all things, yea, the deep things of God. . . . Now we have received, not the spirit of the world, but the spirit which is of God; that we might know the things that are freely given to us of God. Which things also we speak, not in the words which man's wisdom teacheth, but which the Holy Ghost teacheth; comparing spiritual things with spiritual. But the natural man receiveth not the things of the Spirit of God: for they are foolishness unto him: neither can he know them, because they are spiritually discerned" (1 Cor. 2:9-10,12-14).

Now this is a proposition worth testing. The claim here is that, no matter what the "natural man" may get out of the Bible in the way of information or inspiration or instruction, he's missed the "deep things of God," the "things of the Spirit of God." The real communication which threads its way through all the seemingly diverse messages of the sixty-six books of Scripture somehow escapes him. Natural discernment, which functions perfectly well when focused on other books, is of limited value here. Why?

It's because of the Christocentricity of the Bible—to use a six-syllable word which packs far more than six-cylinder power. In simple terms, the Holy Spirit of God authored the Bible to reveal one thing: the redemption that is to be found only through faith in the Son of God. Thus, the "deep things of God" relate to those mysteries concerning Christ's atonement for sin and to the everlasting life which is promised those who repent of their sins and place their trust in him for salvation.

What the Holy Spirit has to say to you and to me through the pages of the Bible is basically this:

1. God is absolute goodness, justice, and holiness, and, therefore, cannot tolerate sin—it would be inconsistent with his nature to allow anything other than purity and innocence to come into his presence.
2. You need a savior, because your spiritual ties to the Creator, who made you in his own image, were severed when sin entered the human race, polluting your own nature and estranging you from God.
3. You can't save yourself, because you must be born again—spiritually, this time—and you are as powerless over your supernatural birth as you were over your natural birth.
4. God, because he loves you regardless of your sinful state, has made a way for you to be spiritually reborn and to come freely into his presence to share eternal fellowship with him rather than to die in your sins.
5. That one way is through repentance and faith in a sinless substitute, Jesus Christ, who was God in human form. He paid the penalty for sin on Calvary and was raised from the dead, thus, purchasing bodily resurrection and eternal life for all those who believe in his name.

Redemption! It's the total message of the Bible. Christ! He's the underlying theme of all the Scriptures. Any por-

tion of the Bible that is difficult to interpret or to understand will invariably make good sense when the redemptive
program of Christ is part of the reader's perspective.

You see what this means? This may come as a shock,
but unless you have experienced this redemption yourself—unless you possess personally a saving knowledge of
Christ in your own life—the Bible can never be interpreted
to your satisfaction. Nor can it ever be genuinely meaningful to you. It says of itself that it was not intended for
natural man, but for spiritual man. Spiritual discernment
is a by-product of spiritual rebirth. It can't be achieved
by any amount of exercising of the frontal lobe.

Take a look at the most accomplished scholar of Christ's
generation, the man to whom He put the simple directive,
"ye must be born again." Nicodemus was bewildered by
the whole idea, and came up with a question unbefitting
even a seven-year-old: "How can a man be born when
he is old? can he enter the second time into his mother's
womb, and be born?" (John 3:4). And after Jesus graciously
overlooked this natural stupidity and patiently explained
spiritual regeneration to him, the intellectual Nicodemus
asked once more in desperation, "How can these things
be?" To which Jesus replied in essence: "Do you mean
to tell me that you are recognized as the national teacher
of Israel and you can't grasp this concept?"

Fortunately for Nicodemus, as for me, God's grace is
sufficient, and he did eventually become a believer. And
you can bet that this man, who was supposed to have been
so knowledgeable in the things of God, began reading his
Bible in an entirely different light after that encounter with
Jesus. He began to read with spiritual discernment.

An even clearer illustration of natural man's inability

to get out of the Bible what it has to offer is afforded by the distinguished figure of a Gentile nobleman, a high-ranking officer of the flourishing kingdom of Ethiopia. He is pictured as being intently engrossed in reading from the book of Isaiah as he sits alone in his royal chariot. Philip, the evangelist, approaches him and asks him if he understands what he's reading. The envoy, obviously an open-minded and good-natured man, says "How can I, except some man should guide me?" (Acts 8:31), and promptly invites Philip to step up in the chariot with him. "Then Philip opened his mouth, and began at the same scripture, and preached unto him Jesus" (Acts 8:35).

Did this make any difference? Immediately after being shown the Christocentric interpretation of the Old Testament prophecy he hadn't been able to figure out by his natural discernment, the ambassador got the message loud and clear. He confessed his utter faith in Jesus Christ as the Son of God, got himself baptized by Philip just three verses later, and went on his way—no longer doubting but "rejoicing."

The fact is proved so conclusively by the existence of one book among the 66 in the Bible—Leviticus. There would be little justification for Leviticus today on grounds that it is history or literature or prophecy or poetry or wisdom or exposition. It is none of these; it is mostly a rule-book of sacrificial and ceremonial practices for a priestly system which hasn't been used by anybody since the time of Christ. To the Jew, Leviticus is now a partially dead book, but for the Christian, it is crammed with fresh new meaning as all its sacerdotal details and purification rites fairly sing of the high priestly role and perfect righteousness of the Savior.

If you'd like to test this for yourself, give yourself one quiet hour out of your schedule. For the first 30 minutes, scan quickly through the 27 chapters of Leviticus and see whether most of its details honestly seem applicable today. Then turn to the New Testament for the remaining 30 minutes and read slowly through the 13 chapters of Hebrews. It is the difference between the lifelessness of extinct ritual and the throbbing power of an eternal new life in Christ. Both marvelously reveal the Savior. It is only because the Bible is Christocentric that it has remained, through the centuries, vibrantly alive in all its parts.

First, Know the Author

Regeneration, then, is the first criterion for learning to read the Bible. I've hinted at this inescapable truth in the past chapters, but from this point on it must be made preeminent, simply because the Bible has far more to say to the Christian than to the unregenerate reader. It is true, of course, that acquaintance with the Scriptures is profitable for moral and ethical and cultural instruction, and that any reader therefore benefits to some degree from continued Bible study. As Dickens wrote to his son, "it is the best book that ever was or ever will be in the world, and . . . it teaches you the best lessons by which any human creature who tries to be truthful and faithful can possibly be guided."

But good conduct and wisdom and virtuous living are only corollary benefits. They are not the fundamental objective toward which the Scriptures are aimed. The Bible, to repeat, is basically a redemptive book, and its whole purpose is to point us toward the Redeemer—the written Word was given to attract us to the living Word.

Consequently, a person who may truly appreciate Bible study and who may conscientiously try to live according to its moral precepts can remain a peripheral reader all his life if he resists the magnetic pull of the Holy Spirit who authored the text, and who strives to draw the reader into a saving knowledge of the Christ of the Bible. To magnify the book and to minimize its Messiah is an incongruity, for the message of both is one and the same.

The Bible is a thoroughly spiritual book which is designed to be spiritually understood. "The Word of God is quick, and powerful, and sharper than any twoedged sword, piercing even to the dividing asunder of soul and spirit, and of the joints and marrow, and is a discerner of the thoughts and intents of the heart" (Heb. 4:12).

There's the clue to perceptive reading: this book is alive and active and is a discerner of your spiritual attitude. If your attitude is one of distrust and doubting, the Holy Spirit discerns that flaw and reveals nothing more to you than is available to any other natural discerner. If your attitude is one of simple faith rooted in personal dependence upon Christ, this discerner of the thoughts and intents of the heart tunes you in to its ultra-high-frequency communication process and your development as a spiritual discerner begins.

Sound mysterious? It certainly is. It's the most marvelous phenomenon I know anything about. I have spent my life with books, and I know of no other system of communication like this, where there is such interchange between author and reader. It's what the psalmist was talking about when he wrote: "The secret of the Lord is with them that fear him; and he will shew them his covenant" (Ps. 25:14).

Primarily, then, the Bible is a textbook for Christians. Like any textbook, it must be approached with a ready assent to its teachings. The child who begins with chapter one of an algebra text doesn't know that he will get predictable results by the time he has finished the book. He simply follows the directions in his text until he arrives at a positive knowledge that the formulas really do work. He knows, because he finds himself obtaining the promised results.

All of us, generally, seem willing to start with unquestioning faith in the directions given by textbooks. It never occurs to us to suspect them unless we happen to discover sometime afterward that they are untrustworthy. The Bible asks no more—just follow its instructions, believing that they will produce the promised results, and then you will know for yourself.

First faith, then knowledge. At no point along the way to becoming an intelligent Bible reader are we expected to set reason aside and accept even one illogical premise. With faith preceding reason, we find God's Word to be as rational as it is spiritual, and never requiring any fanciful interpretations. The Lord doesn't say, "Come now, and let us imagine together," but "Come now, and let us reason together" (Isa. 1:18).

Unintelligent notions about what the Bible says have certainly been spread around in profusion, but we are warned that such would be the case. Peter tells us plainly of "some things hard to be understood" in the writings of Paul, "which they that are unlearned and unstable wrest, as they do also the other scriptures" (2 Pet. 3:16). Consequently he advises the reader to be always on the alert, "Knowing this first, that no prophecy of the scripture is of any private interpretation" (2 Pet. 1:20).

Applying this combination of absolute dependence on the power of faith coupled with full utilization of the power of reason enables us to read the Bible with 20-20 vision, and to avoid such errors in understanding. Let's put on these bifocals and have a clear look at some of the more troublesome aspects of Bible study which are the usual spawning grounds for misinterpretation and doubting.

Do I Have to Believe in Miracles?

Unequivocally yes. But please delay your reaction until you have read the next ten paragraphs.

The Bible reports many miraculous events which cause us to wonder greatly, which stagger our credulity. How can we believe unreservedly that the sun stopped in its course for Joshua to complete a battle, that Elisha caused iron to "swim," that Jesus restored life to a putrefying corpse four days after the burial? Or does each miracle yield to explanation in terms which are entirely within the acceptable limits of natural phenomena and scientific inquiry?

In order to get at the heart of the answer, let's conceive of miracles as falling into three categories: (1) mechanical, (2) natural, and (3) supernatural.

We encounter no difficulty with the first of these. We frankly marvel at the transmission of telephoto pictures in color, printed in your morning newspaper within a matter of minutes after they were snapped at the scene of the event in Buenos Aires or Calcutta or Rome. The electronic arm which responds to the amputee's brain impulses, even down to the minute movements of artificial fingers, is a marvel indeed. The spacecraft which flashes information by telemetry from the moon at the rate of

15,200 items per second—enough new knowledge to fill
a standard-size encyclopedia every hour—is a miraculous
achievement. The computer which can store 4,000 trillion
bits of data in its memory bank, compared with the one-
trillion capacity of the human brain, makes us shake our
heads in disbelief.

These mechanical miracles can be explained—some of
them are nothing more than lights and wires in a box—but
this hardly minimizes their amazing performance. As creatures of the inventive genius of man, they ought to demonstrate to all the validity of God's promise to his own creature that he would put the mysteries of nature under his
dominion. God has placed no limits on human ability to
harness and channel and package these energy sources of
the natural environment, and Jesus, the greatest mira-
cle-worker of all, may have been thinking of twentieth-
century man when he remarked that "greater works than
these shall he do" (John 14:12). The hand of God is manifest in every mechanical miracle ever devised, simply because he invented the inventor.

Natural miracles, of course, surround us on all sides
and become visible in ever-increasing quantity and scope
as we discover more about our universe. The fantastic
world of activity inside every cell is just being opened up
to us by the newer ultramicroscopes. We never knew until
recent decades about the fixed chromosome code-patterns
for each species of life, or the ballet-like motions of the
800 million genes locked inside each chromosome during
the miraculous growth process called mitosis. Not until
tape recordings were made of the natural magnetic radia-
tions emitted by celestial bodies as they plummet through
space were we aware that each has its own "signature

music," or identifying vibrations that are unique and distinct from all others. But God's Word has hinted for more than 1,900 years that we would some day discover this marvel: "There is one glory of the sun, and another glory of the moon, and another glory of the stars: for one star differeth from another star in glory" (1 Cor. 15:41).

We can expect all natural miracles eventually to yield to satisfactory explanation as knowledge expands. It took a long time for man to understand what caused the eerie apparition of "St. Elmo's Fire" which awed generations of seamen. I have seen this strange luminescence limning the masts and rigging and lines of more than one ship, and I can tell you that it is still an awesome experience for any seafarer on a dark night in the rolling deep. Other phenomena, like the efficient communication system of the honey bee, whose dance gives the rest of the hive specific data in terms of direction and distance to the source of nectar in some far-off flower field, remain a mystery to the scientific mind.

In the areas of mechanical and natural miracles, I believe that the philosophy of Ulysses is our birthright: "to strive, to seek, to find, and not to yield." But supernatural miracles draw us into a completely new dimension. When the Bible tells us that Jesus fed 5,000 people with what was originally a supply of two dried fishes and five rolls, with twelve basketfuls left over after the picnic, we must yield either to doubt or to belief that the Lord of nature was demonstrating his authority over it in an utterly miraculous way.

Some of the miracles reported in the Bible might lend themselves to rationalization. God could use natural events to communicate to his people, just as he does today. His angel of death that decimated the Assyrian army laying siege to Jerusalem could very plausibly represent bubonic plague or some other pestilence. The extension of King Hezekiah's life by fifteen years could have been the natural arrest of a physiological condition.

But many of the great wonders of the Scriptures do not leave the slightest option for purely natural explanation. The Red Sea crossing was a supernaturally directed event as the Bible presents it, and not a mere fording by the fleeing Israelites of a shallow marsh which somehow the whole Egyptian army lacked the strategy to negotiate. Either Jesus walked on the surface of a storm-tossed Sea of Galilee twenty-five or thirty furlongs (three or four miles) from the shore, as reported in the sixth chapter of the book of John—or he didn't. Faith preceding reason allows us to accept without question all the mighty works of God.

It is not reasonable to expect that we can always discover facts to substantiate the supernatural miracles reported in the Scriptures, but occasionally this is true. A fascinating instance has to do with the stupendous event which occurred during Joshua's campaign against the Amorite forces: "Then spake Joshua to the Lord in the day when the Lord delivered up the Amorites before the children of Israel, and he said in the sight of Israel, Sun, stand thou still upon Gibeon; and thou, Moon, in the valley of Ajalon. And the sun stood still, and the moon stayed, until the people had avenged themselves upon their enemies. Is not this written in the book of Jasher? So the sun stood still in the midst of heaven, and hasted not to go down about a whole day. And there was no day like that before it or after it, that the Lord hearkened unto the voice of a man: for the Lord fought for Israel" (Josh.

10:12-14).

Whether God performed this miracle through the re-
fraction of light rays or by a sudden tilt of the earth's
axis, or by an alteration in the rate of rotation, we don't
know. But we do know that ancient Chinese writings during
the reign of Emperor Yeo, thought to be a contemporary
of Joshua, make mention of a long day unlike any other.
And we are told by the Greek historian, Herodotus, that
the priests of Egypt showed him in the fifth century B.C.,
the record of such a day in their computations which had
been kept by generations of Egyptian astronomers.

The story is told that, shortly before 1900, a British
astronomer, Sir Edwin Ball, conducted scientific research
on solar time for the past few thousand years, and reported
that his calculations could not account for 24 hours of
astronomic movement. About the same time, Professor
C. A. Totten of Yale University, and a fellow scientist who
was a religious skeptic, became interested in this discrepancy in the calendar. Totten reported that his colleague's
research revealed a shortage of exactly 23 hours and 20
minutes in the computation tables. Totten suggested that
his friend consult the early biblical record as part of his
continuing search for clues to the lost time.

When the skeptic came across this passage in Joshua,
he was astounded to find such a reference, but pointed
out to Totten that this proved the inaccuracy of the Scriptures, because only 23 hours and 20 minutes could be
accounted for. Totten, a Christian, reminded him that the
Bible says specifically "about a whole day," and suggested
that he continue his reading, which he did, until he came
to this report of the sign which God gave to Hezekiah
in Isaiah 38:8: "Behold, I will bring again the shadow of

the degrees, which is gone down in the sun dial of Ahaz, ten degrees backward. So the sun returned ten degrees, by which degrees it was gone down."

Now anybody who has a sundial knows that ten degrees on the dial is 40 minutes on a clock face. That gave the scientist his answer to the missing 24 hours in his figures. And I imagine it made a believer out of him, because without the Bible there still would be no answer to this scientific puzzle. But if God chooses not to let us have any of the facts confirming his miracles, we can still believe them. It makes a lot more sense to trust his Word from the front end than to spend our lives trying to back into some understanding of it based on what man is able to put together.

The climax of all miracles, the resurrection of Jesus Christ, puts the whole question of supernatural intervention in its proper perspective. If you can not give assent to God's power over death, then you don't know the omnipotent God of the Bible. The Creator who conceived, established, and revealed to humanity his natural laws is able to set aside, suspend, or alter those laws at any time and any place in any way he might choose.

In other words, it all goes back to the reader's spiritual attitude. When you read in the sixth chapter of 2 Kings about the lost axhead which Elisha caused to float to the surface of the stream simply by throwing a small piece of wood into the water near the spot, you could conclude that this was a trivial and even ludicrous employment of the prophet's miraculous powers. But if you read with spiritual discernment, inviting the Holy Spirit to reveal to you the Christocentric message of his Word, this is what you see:

The law of gravitation caused the iron to sink.
Because iron is heavier than water or wood, the
ax sank. Into the stick Elisha cast into the water
a new force was introduced giving it a greater
attractive power. Thus it became as strong as a
magnet and overcame the attraction of gravitation
and its hidden power brought the iron to the surface. Do we not have here another type of Christ?
Was he not the "Branch" (Zech. 3:8; 6:12) who
was cut down and who, because he descended into
the waters of death for us, is now able to raise
us up into the air of heaven and restore us to our
Owner for his use? This beautifully acted parable,
says old Trapp, teaches us that "God can as easily
make our hard, heavy hearts, sunk down in the
world's mud, to float upon life's stream and see
heaven again." [1]

It really takes no great step of faith to believe every
miracle catalogued in the Bible, and it is an absolutely
essential step. Those who are skeptical of miracles have
placed their faith in a limited deity, rather than in the
one who says, "Behold, I am the Lord, the God of all
flesh: is there any thing too hard for me?" (Jer. 32:27).
Whether we can understand and explain all the hows
and whys is not the most important consideration. It is
thoroughly logical, when confronted by God's supernatural
acts either in the written record or in our daily lives, to
lean on him for those things which are beyond our capacity
to reason—at least until God, in his providential wisdom,
enlarges our reasoning power and reveals the explanation
of such mysteries to us. This is the explicit advice of the

Bible: "Trust in the Lord with all thine heart; and lean not unto thine own understanding. In all thy ways acknowledge him, and he shall direct thy paths" (Prov. 3:5-6).

After all, a miracle has been described as "the simplicity of faith coupled with the sufficiency of God's omnipotence." If you are unwilling to trust and obey, wouldn't you have to doubt the power of a miracle-working God?

Am I Supposed to Take the Bible Literally, or Figuratively?

Both.

The Bible is literature, and as such it contains generous mixtures of literal language and figures of speech, just as our daily communication does. Ordinary intelligence is usually the key to whether the passage is intended as a statement of fact or as a symbolic expression. When Hosea advises the Israelites to "break up your fallow ground" (Hos. 10:12), it should be obvious to all but the most unenlightened that he is using the words metaphorically to mean "stir up your dulled conscience." The Apocalypse, or book of Revelation, is almost entirely symbolistic writing.

But the safest rule to follow is to take God at his word. He says exactly what he means and means exactly what he says. Most of the time, no matter what secondary significations the terms may bear, a serpent is a serpent, a plow is a plow, an evil spirit is an evil spirit. Assume the literal meaning unless it is clear that an allegorical sense is strongly indicated. Rest in the assurance that God will never direct you through his Word to do anything wrong, anything foolish, anything hurtful to others. If some Bible "scholar" tries to persuade you that a passage of Scripture suggests or condones such behavior, you can know that he has misread his Bible. As pointed out in the beginning of this chapter, "the natural man receiveth not the things of the Spirit of God: for they are foolishness unto him: neither can he know them, because they are spiritually discerned" (1 Cor. 2:14).

The Garden of Eden, for instance, can not be mythologized as just a clever word picture of original innocence. It is presented to us as a tangible geographic location, pinpointed not far from where the Tigris and Euphrates rivers flow together. Adam's name is a variant of the word for "earth," and, therefore, simply means "earthling"—but the Bible repeatedly lists him in genealogies as an identifiable person, having children with the names of Cain and Abel and Seth born to him and his wife, Eve. I believe in this original family, not as mere representations of the beginnings of mankind, but as flesh-and-blood people who did the things reported of them in the book of Genesis.

The Flood, whether you consider it localized to the known world of Mesopotamia or global in scope, is literally acceptable to researchers who have probed into the evidence—geological, archaeological, and documentary. Jesus, in his solemn reference to the story of Jonah and the whale, cast no doubt whatever on the actuality of events as described in the Old Testament; neither can I. Heaven and hell are realities of which the Bible gives meager descriptions; but no room is permitted for doubting that they are literal situations, with deliberate, fixed roles in God's eternal plan.

It is a mistake to try to "spiritualize" the original meaning away from the words in an effort to draw more from the text than it was intended to convey. Israel always refers to the chosen nation of the eastern Mediterranean world, and not to the church or some spiritual entity. Egypt, the Red Sea, the Wilderness of Sinai, and the Promised Land of Canaan might be used to visualize (1) enslavement in sin; (2) salvation and baptism; (3) the desert of doubt and rebellion; and (4) the victorious life or sanctification. But their literal nature remains unaffected by these figurative applications. They were as real when first mentioned, of course, as they are today.

Wouldn't you have to agree that Winston Churchill, on whom history has conferred the title of "man of the century," was a reasonable and pragmatic person? He certainly could not be considered gullible. Listen to what Churchill had to say on this very subject:

"We believe that the most scientific view, the most up-to-date and rational conception, will find its fullest satisfaction in taking the Bible story literally. We may be sure that all these things happened just as they are set out according to Holy Writ. We may believe that they happened to people not so very different from ourselves, and that the impressions those people received were faithfully recorded, and have been transmitted across the centuries with far more accuracy than many of the telegraphed accounts we read of goings on today."

What one contemporary writer calls "the golden rule of interpretation which the biblical record of fulfilled prophecy indicates is correct" is expressed this way: "When the plain sense of Scripture makes common sense, seek no other sense; therefore take every word at its primary, ordinary, usual, literal meaning unless the facts of the immediate context, studied in the light of related passages and axiomatic and fundamental truths, indicate clearly otherwise." [2]

Peter admonishes us to avoid any rash assumptions when he reminds us that "we have not followed cunningly devised fables, when we made known unto you the power and coming of our Lord Jesus Christ, but were eyewitnesses of his majesty" (2 Pet. 1:16). The inspired writers knew that human attempts would be made to allegorize the literal portions of the message radiated through them by the Holy Spirit. The Bible is to be read with a faith that is intelligent and with an intelligence that is faithful. This approach allows room for neither fanciful writing nor fanciful interpretation.

Can Bible Passages Be Quoted Out of Context and Still Make Good Sense?

A favorite device of skeptics for centuries has been the practice of taking Scripture out of context to make it appear silly or self-contradictory. Just by selective editing, you can come up with a prophecy that ostriches will some day appreciate irrigation, or "prove" that Moses broke all Ten Commandments at one time, or discover a king hunting a flea, or find five automobile parts listed in a single chapter, or read of a man getting indigestion from eating a little book, or produce "evidence" of God getting tired.

The customary example of this kind of irreverent fakery is to cite the fact that the Bible states "There is no God." It does say that, but in the context of the sentence, "The fool hath said in his heart, There is no God" (Ps. 14:1), and only a fool would read it out of this context. Similarly, the following Christian guideline may be quoted as a justification for licentious living: "All things are lawful unto me." That is true, but Paul's full statement is: "All things are lawful unto me, but I will not be brought under the power of any" (1 Cor. 6:12). Quite a different evaluation of the freedom which God's grace allows!

The appropriate frame of reference is essential to our understanding of many portions of Scripture which otherwise could leave us with a totally wrong impression. Ecclesiastes is filled with the language of despair, and in places it reads like a suicide note: "Therefore I hated life; because the work that is wrought under the sun is grievous unto me: for all is vanity and vexation of spirit" (2:17). Actually, the entire book is a reflection of the shocking misery of the backslider out of fellowship with God, and not until its final conclusion does it sound the note of victory: "Fear God, and keep his commandments: for this is the whole duty of man" (12:13).

When we allow for the Song of Solomon being an Oriental love poem, we are not discomfited by such imagery as this: "Behold, thou art fair, my love; behold, thou art fair; thou hast doves' eyes within thy locks: thy hair is as a flock of goats, that appear from mount Gilead. Thy teeth are like a flock of sheep that are even shorn, which came up from the washing; whereof every one bear twins, and none is barren among them. Thy lips are like a thread of scarlet, and thy speech is comely: thy temples are like a piece of pomegranate within thy locks. Thy neck is like the tower of David builded for an armoury, whereon there hang a thousand bucklers, all shields of mighty men" (4:1-4). Quoted out of the format of the rest of the poem, the words tend to take on a comical connotation.

Lack of familiarity with the laws and customs of a primitive Oriental society can do violence to an appreciation of the story of Ruth. The codes governing betrothal and property required that she lie at the feet of a strange man as he slept on his threshing floor. Our Western minds have difficulty accommodating such a concept to the standards of innocence and modesty, just as they do with the idea that the Japanese code provided a high degree of privacy in mixed public bathing.

But another passage from the same book is almost always quoted out of context, without losing any of its sublime meaning: "Intreat me not to leave thee, or to return from following after thee: for whither thou goest, I will go; and where thou lodgest, I will lodge: thy people shall be my people, and thy God my God" (Ruth 1:16). This beloved pledge heard so often at wedding ceremonies expresses the highest level of human devotion—even though it was originally spoken not by bride and groom but by a pagan widow to her godly mother-in-law.

Again, the familiar Mizpah which generations of Christians have recited at times of separation, "The Lord watch between me and thee, when we are absent one from another" (Gen. 31:49), is almost always used out of context with the portion of Scripture in which it occurs. The original Mizpah was a heap of stones erected by Jacob and his scheming father-in-law, Laban, as a point of demarcation to signal the end of twenty years of mutual cheating and conniving which the two had perpetrated against each other. Here are Laban's words: "This heap be witness, and this pillar be witness, that I will not pass over this heap to thee, and that thou shalt not pass over this heap and this pillar unto me, for harm" (Gen. 31:52). But out of context or not, the Mizpah is a perennial blessing, authored and preserved by the Holy Spirit for believers.

And that's the point that needs to be made forcefully: the Bible is God's Word—all of it is God speaking. Therefore, many nuggets of truth can be abstracted from their time and setting and applied universally or to particular circumstances. With the consummate skill of a master teacher, Jesus constantly drew short phrases and sentences from the Old Testament, preceding them with "It is written" and applying them to specific incidents and conditions in his day. He taught that we are to live by every word that proceeds out of the mouth of God. As far as I am concerned, there is no more quotable volume in all the world than the Bible.

After all, what is it you really want? Isn't *learning* one of your sincerest goals? And wouldn't you say that *hope* is one thing your life has to include if it is to be worth living? Well, grab a firm hold on this truth right now: whatever the Bible says is designed to add to your learning and to strengthen your hope. This discovery was made more than nineteen centuries ago by a thinker whose intellectual powers surpassed those of the famed philosophers of his time, and whose heroic endurance in the face of overwhelming opposition is without equal in human history. Paul's words assure us that "Whatsoever things were written aforetime were written for our learning, that we through patience and comfort of the scriptures might have hope" (Rom. 15:4).

Wrongly used, of course, the so-called "proof-text method" of argumentation is reprehensible. But as long as we read with spiritual discernment, we aren't going to be using Scripture out of context, even though we may apply it in a completely new way. Whenever God's message fits the situation, then truly "a word fitly spoken is like apples of gold in pictures of silver" (Prov. 25:11).

What's the Best Way to Get Started?

From a strictly human point of view, it might be argued that "inspiration is 90 percent perspiration." It's not quite that way with Bible study, but certainly there is some work involved, and a planned approach can be of great help toward becoming a knowledgeable student of the Scriptures. Here are some suggested procedures that will be of practical help to you.

(1) *Make a place for the Bible in your daily schedule.* Get dogmatic about reserving a half-hour somewhere in each day's affairs to get off with yourself and your Bible, otherwise you'll find it's the easiest item on your agenda to postpone or skip completely. Find a quiet time when you can study without distractions, and hold to a regular schedule in order to build up a continuity of research. You will be amazed at how the Bible's teachings begin to "fall together" into a continuous, interwoven stream of ideas which once seemed to be entirely unrelated to each other. You can't expect hit-or-miss reading to draw you into this flow of eternal truth; you'll have to make the Bible an integral part of your daily living.

(2) *Get a Bible you are comfortable with.* Some editions are in large print, with plain pages unbroken by marginal notes or typographical devices of any kind. Others can be purchased which offer a wide variety of incorporated study helps: footnotes, chronological tables, maps, outlines of each book, colored maps and pictures, chain references, all the words of Christ printed in red ink, etc. You'll find that some editions are ornate and imaginative, but not very suitable for serious study. A bride's Bible, for example, is designed primarily to look pretty in a wedding ceremony. Get the book in whatever format appeals to you most.

(3) *Don't be afraid to look at more than one version.* If

you find a passage difficult to understand because of the language used, try reading it in another translation or revision. My personal preference, as stated before, is the King James (or Authorized) Version. I consider it to be not only the most beautifully translated but also the most trustworthy, as God has obviously blessed it through the centuries.

But if I find Proverbs 11:15, for example, hard to interpret: "He that is surety for a stranger shall smart for it; and he that hateth suretiship is sure," I can try The Amplified Old Testament version "He who becomes security for an outsider shall smart for it, but he who hates suretiship is secure from its penalties." If it is still unclear, I may read it in The Paraphrased Books of the Bible, published by the Billy Graham Association: "Be sure you know a person well before you vouch for his credit! Better refuse than suffer later." Then I look once more at the King James rendering, and "He that is surety for a stranger shall smart for it; and he that hateth suretiship is sure" reads more smoothly.

Unless you have made a thorough study of the circumstances under which some of the contemporary versions of the Scriptures have been produced, it is wise to depend on the tested versions whose fidelity to the original manuscripts has been established. But it can be enlightening to compare with others the wording of passages whose meaning may be obscure in the version which you are reading.

(4) *Develop the habit of using a concordance.* Many Bibles include an abbreviated concordance, or index, but these are generally too limited for thorough study. With

an exhaustive work like *Young's Analytical Concordance* available, you are quickly referred to every place in the Bible that any word occurs and you are given all the meanings of the original Hebrew and Greek roots. Since words represent thoughts, the concordance becomes a key to unlocking some of the most remarkable discoveries you will ever make.

Let's take just one case. The Sixth Commandment says: "Thou shalt not kill" (Ex. 20:13). Does this mean that all Christians should be conscientious objectors when confronted with military service, or that they are automatically condemned if they should happen to kill an armed intruder in the home before he can carry out a family massacre? What does the word *kill* mean?

Your concordance shows you there are ten words in the Hebrew which mean "kill": *harag, zabach, chalal, tabach, muth, nakah, nagaph, qatal, scachat,* and *ratsach.* Their various meanings include "to slay, to slaughter, to pierce, to put to death, to smite, to sacrifice"; but only one of the ten, *ratsach,* means specifically "to murder." In the Greek, there are six words for "kill": *anaireo, apokteino, diacheirizomai, thuo, sphatto,* and *phoneuo.* All mean "to kill" or "to sacrifice," but *phoneuo* is reserved for "to murder." The Sixth Commandment, and all references to it in both the Old and New Testaments, make pointed use of only the Hebrew *ratsach* and the Greek *phoneuo.*

The Commandment, in other words, is "Thou shalt not murder," which involves killing as an act of passion, hatred, or premeditation. Jesus, commenting on this matter, made it clear that hatred and lust in the heart are the same as assault and murder in God's sight, whether killing takes place or not. It makes a "world" of difference when we know what the words are saying.

(5) *Enlarge your study by consulting books about the Bible.* Some editions, like the Scofield Bible, attempt to furnish background information and explanations of key passages along with the scriptural text. More helpful are the commentaries, which may give verse-by-verse exegesis and interpretation. My favorite is *Matthew Henry's Commentary.* It is thoroughly reverent, highly practical, and usually doctrinally sound. In my opinion, others may be more readable but inclined toward unscriptural interpretations, and, therefore, should be selected with care.

There are, of course, books devoted to every aspect of Bible study. Handbooks, like *Halley's Bible Handbook* and Mears' *What the Bible Is All About,* summarize and organize data for quick reference; Robertson's *A Harmony of the Gospels* unravels and coordinates the confusing progression of events as reported by the first four New Testament books; these are invaluable study helps. A Greek-English diaglott, or line-by-line transliteration of the New Testament, can be very useful for comparative analysis. A Bible atlas gives fuller understanding of the places especially significant in the unfolding history of redemption. Finally, a Bible dictionary is as indispensable as *Webster's* or *Funk & Wagnall's* for general study.

As your interest grows, you will become acquainted with an ever-widening circle of books and pamphlets and magazines which explore Bible truths in a scholarly and unbiased way. And don't forget the news media. Current daily events frequently dovetail precisely with what the Bible has to say about this gospel age, and without forcing analogies or manipulating Scriptures you will begin to relate the "signs of the times" to the Bible message in a most meaningful new light.

But a word of caution here: let the object of your concentration always remain the same—God's Word. Often, what man has to say about what God has to say generates more heat than light. The focus must be kept unswervingly on the truth as expressed in the Bible, whether it is entirely clear to us or not. Everything is to be tested against God's Word. The Christians at Berea were evidently of the very highest type, because we read that they double-checked even the statements of Paul against the absolute standard: "These were more noble than those in Thessalonica, in that they received the word with all readiness of mind, and searched the scriptures daily, whether those things were so" (Acts 17:11).

Learning to read, then, is a fascinating process, a lifelong adventure. The rewards increase as you mine deeper and deeper into the hidden riches and discover, for yourself alone, one jewel after another to enrich your spiritual life. First, you must meet the Author—after that, you're bound to find new meaning that you never dreamed his Book contained, when you read it before you knew him. How much you get out of the Bible will be measured in direct proportion to how diligently and earnestly you seek to appropriate, live by, and share its message.

"Study to shew thyself approved unto God, a workman that needeth not to be ashamed, rightly dividing the word of truth" (2 Tim. 2:15). As you do, you will begin to see why this book is truly "alive and powerful." You can't read it without realizing that, of all the volumes ever written, this one alone is reading you.

---

[1] Herbert Lockyer, *All the Miracles of the Bible:* (Grand Rapids: Zondervan Publishing House, 1961), pp. 187-88. Used by permission.

[2] Hal Lindsey with C. C. Carlson, *The Late Great Planet Earth,* Zondervan Publishing House, Grand Rapids, Michigan, 1971, quoting from David L. Cooper, *When God's Armies Meet the Almighty in the Land of Israel,* Biblical Research Society, Los Angeles, 1940.

9.
THE BIBLE—WHO NEEDS IT?

The Bible may not add years to your life, but it will add life to your years.

Of all the questions which have been raised so far in this book, by far the easiest to answer is the one appearing in the chapter title above.

Who needs the Bible? I do.

I need the Bible because I am a pragmatist. I have to have something that works, something that can be depended on to function whenever the occasion demands, something that means business when I do. As a finite creature, I need this three-dimensional instrument that I can see, and hold in my hands, and put to productive use like a tool.

I need the Bible because I am a learner. I want to know about such elusive realities as eternity, sin, salvation, bodily resurrection, everlasting life, the glories of heaven, the finality of hell. The Bible talks to me in terms I can relate to, where theology and philosophy lead me into endless circles of speculation. I find that it sifts out the error, the half-truths, the equivocation, and leaves for me that solid truth I can get my teeth into.

I need the Bible because it gives me a trustworthy system

of priorities. It allows me the privilege of forming my own value judgments or of consulting all other sources for facts and opinions; but it remains the unfailing standard by which all truth can be measured.

It simplifies for me all the complexities involved in the quest for life's direction and purpose: "But seek ye first the kingdom of God, and his righteousness; and all these things shall be added unto you" (Matt. 6:33).

I need the Bible because I am conscious of my pilgrim-status. It is obvious to me that all things about me are caught up in the process of change. Like Abraham, I recognize that I am in transit, and that here I have no continuing city. Therefore, I need a road map so that I can be sure of where I'm going. The Bible doesn't provide me with an exact timetable, but it charts my course as surely as the navigational instructions that I once depended on to get me to the other side of the globe and back home again. Written in the language of timelessness, it prepares me for the temporal changes which are but stepping-stones to eternity.

I need the Bible because I am a child of this world. It alerts me to temptation, protects me from the charlatan, immunizes me against environmental ennui, rebukes me for backsliding, and steers my feet along the road to heaven. It is the only rule of conduct I require, for it tells me how to trust, how to forgive, how to worship, how to be a good citizen, how to endure. As Gregory expressed it, "The Scriptures teach us the best way of living, the noblest way of suffering, and the most comfortable way of dying."

I need the Bible because I am a child of God. I need to be informed of what God has to say to me—not once-for-all, but from day to day. One of the marvels of this Book is the fact that, although it was written in the earliest days of antiquity, and hasn't been added to for about twenty centuries, the words are addressed to me and to you right now. The promise of God, 3,500 years ago, that "all the families of the earth" (Gen. 12:3) would be blessed through a people that he would call out to be his chosen nation is fulfilled to us by the irrefutable evidence of the gift of this Bible which has come to us as a result of that promise. How wonderfully relevant today are the words written in the otherwise remote past: "Whatsoever things were written aforetime were written for our learning, that we through patience and comfort of the scriptures might have hope" (Rom. 15:4).

I need the Bible because proper nourishment is essential to spiritual growth, just as it is to physical development. The growing child needs, first milk, then meat. "As new-born babes, desire the sincere milk of the word, that ye may grow thereby" (1 Pet. 2:2). But after we have tasted that the Lord is gracious, in Peter's words, we want to move on to the solid food that brings maturity: "For every one that useth milk is unskilful in the word of righteousness: for he is a babe. But strong meat belongeth to them that are of full age, even those who by reason of use have their senses exercised to discern both good and evil" (Heb. 5:13-14). The Bible is food, and my spirit can no more manage without it on a regular basis than my body can function without scheduled mealtimes.

Getting Personal

The point I strive to make is this: the Bible is an intensely personal book. That's the reason for these frankly personal references, and for those that follow. The Bible talks to me about the ordinary problems and affairs of daily living, just as a close friend would. But there have been critical periods or momentous experiences in my life when God's Word communicated to me in a most unforgettable manner.

One of the first really dramatic demonstrations I had of the peculiar power of Scripture to hit home with the message occurred during World War II when I was serving aboard a troop landing ship. This was the amphibious workhorse of the Pacific fleet, designated by the Navy as the *LST* and dubbed by the crews as "long slow target." Our convoy had slipped out of Leyte Gulf about midnight en route to Mindoro Island for an invasion which was to bottle up the Japanese command in Manila. We had passed through the Surigao Strait and into the mid-Philippine waterway leading to the Sulu Sea when the first air attack came.

I was a veteran of three years of warfare at sea and was no stranger to opposition from submarines and planes. But as the Vals and Zekes began to pick out their targets in the convoy of about 60 ships, I suddenly realized that this was a different game. These pilots were not even attempting to pull out of their bombing dives and strafing runs, but were transforming themselves into missiles aimed at our ships. This previously unstructured experience of watching humans commit suicide with their machines— regardless of the fact that some of them missed their targets—filled me with a sense of revulsion and terror, as though I were in the presence of something more sinister and evil than I had ever before been near.

As I watched stricken tankers exploding into orange balls

of fire and *LST*'s breaking in half at the impact of bomb-laden planes, I recall vividly the moment when a "bogey" spiraled down out of the clouds and picked out our file of ships, dodging collective streams of antiaircraft fire as it skimmed low over the long line of masts behind us. "Is this it?" I gasped inwardly, as I felt the confrontation with sudden death only seconds away.

At that instant the Japanese plane dropped into the main deck of the ship directly behind us—a huge Dutch freighter carrying a full cargo of ammunition. The resulting explosion was a cataclysm of sight and sound, but the ensuing silence seemed even more awesome. The kamikaze attack was over as abruptly as it had started. A grey-black canopy of smoke and gases—all that was left of what seconds before was a 48,000-ton ship and its crew—enveloped the entire convoy like a shroud. I stood there speechless, like every other man on topside, gazing at the emptiness behind and the pall overhead and wondering when the frozen grip in my throat would release itself.

Then, over the ship's public address system came the words, recited, I presume, by a chaplain. I didn't know whose the voice was, but I knew Whose the words were: "The Lord is my shepherd; I shall not want. . . . He restoreth my soul. . . . Yea, though I walk through the valley of the shadow of death, I will fear no evil; for thou art with me; thy rod and thy staff they comfort me. . . . Surely goodness and mercy shall follow me all the days of my life" (Ps. 23:1,3-4,6).

I can tell you that no food ever nourished my body more effectively than God's assurances of care and comfort and goodness and mercy fed to my soul at that ugly moment when the horror of war closed in on me. Because

this was for real—with the menacing slopes of enemy-held
Negros Island on one side and Tagolo's hostile promontory
on the other, and the scene and smell of destruction all
around, I was in a literal "valley of the shadow of death,"
where I was in genuine spiritual need. But the words—they
were God's, and their promise was effectual, because I
was soon fearing no evil. And despite the fact that, in
the next few days before we were to complete our mission,
50 or 60 more kamikaze encounters were to follow on the
heels of the first, I found myself positively fortified and
sustained by the power of the Holy Spirit which had flowed
through the medium of the written and spoken word into
my needy soul.

Psychosomatic, you say? A semantic overreaction? An
adrenalin response triggered by the fear mechanism? Or
perhaps just a crutch for lame courage? Call it what you
will, it filled a desperate void deep down where I live.
I could "identify" in that moment with one of the most
fearless warriors and one of the greatest men of faith in
all history, David the Israelite who confessed: "But I am
poor and needy; yet the Lord thinketh upon me: thou
art my help and my deliverer" (Ps. 40:17).

Whether it's one of life's major crises we face, or just
the steady eroding influences of daily living, it's this personal confrontation with God in the Bible that makes all
the difference. The Bible was written for you, just as though
your name were inscribed on it. Where any other book
allows you to remain disinterested and neutral, this one
demands your reaction, your involvement.

The only way you can keep the Bible from reaching
you with its personal message is to avoid it altogether.
It tells you unequivocally that "whatsoever is not of faith

is sin" (Rom. 14:23). That's quite an inclusive statement—it means that if you choose to reject God's Word instead of listening to what it has to say and committing yourself fully to it, you are sinning. And because God rewards unremitted sin in like kind, you are, therefore, choosing between blessing and cursing, between life and death. The old aphorism that "sin keeps the Bible away and the Bible keeps sin away" is more than a trite slogan.

Get Acquainted

Knowing a lot about the Bible isn't the same thing as having a personal confrontation. I have known *about* the Holy Land for most of my lifetime. But only since I began the writing of this book have I come to *know* the Holy Land, because I visited it in person, and thereby—for the first time—gained a personal knowledge of it. In a similar way, I knew *about* a former President, Harry S. Truman, but after working with him in person as a researcher and writer for his memoirs throughout most of 1954 in Kansas City, I could accurately say that I *knew* the ex-President.

David, the only man in the Scriptures described as "a man after God's heart," knew the Bible. If you want to see how much the Bible can mean to an individual on the personal level, read the inspired words of David. He didn't have anything but the Torah (the law), but he fed on every word of it. For example, you can skim through Psalm 119 and count 176 statements of praise for the Bible, which David refers to variously as "thy commandments," "thy Word," "thy testimonies," "thy law," "thy statutes, ' "thy judgments," "thy ordinances," "thy precepts," and "thy ways." By substituting the word, "Bible," for each one of these synonyms, you'll find David singing:

O, how I love thy law [Bible] (v. 97).

My soul breaketh for the longing that it hath unto thy judgments [Bible] (v. 20).

Wherewithal shall a young man cleanse his way? By taking heed thereto according to thy word [Bible] (v. 9).

I have more understanding than all my teachers: for thy testimonies [Bible] are my meditation (v. 99).

I hate and abhor lying; but thy law [Bible] do I love (v. 163).

Great peace have they which love thy law [Bible]: and nothing shall offend them (v. 165).

Thy word [Bible] is true from the beginning (v. 160).

Depart from me, ye evildoers: for I will keep the commandments [Bible] of my God (v. 115).

So shall I have wherewith to answer him that reproacheth me: for I trust in thy word [Bible] (v. 42).

David loved the Bible, not because he was a good man (he was a murderer and an adulterer) but because he found forgiveness and met God on his terms, through his Word. He knew what the Bible could do for him personally. The converted drunkard may not know as much about the Word as the seminarian; but if he has found a new life in Christ, a reformed pattern of living, and eternal peace and security, then he has had a confrontation with the message of the Bible, and he knows what it has done for him.

To the leering skeptic who offers the shallow observation

that no one should depend on a crutch, I reply with enthusiasm: if knowledge is a crutch, I'll take a pair. With the New Testament holding me up on one side I can manage to stand; but with the Old Testament on the other side I have all wisdom under my feet and am ready to walk—"do not my words do good to him that walketh uprightly?" (Mic. 2:7).

Not depend on the Bible for support? To me, it is a corneal transplant, without which my vision would still be clouded: "One thing I know, that, whereas I was blind, now I see" (John 9:25). It is my "pacemaker" which the cardiologist implants in the chest to keep the heart beating true, because "the heart is deceitful above all things, and desperately wicked: who can know it?" (Jer. 17:9).

God's message characterizes itself as a sword that pierces the believer's conscience and smites his enemies; a judge that calls us to account daily; a lamp that dispels the darkness from our understanding; a mirror that enables us to see ourselves as God sees us; a laver that cleanses and refreshes; a fire that burns out the dross of sin; a hammer that breaks down the stubborn will; and a seed to be scattered bountifully that it might produce much fruit.

Learn from History

Take a lesson from the nations. Israel, which has always honored God's Word, is still with us despite the unending efforts of world empires to wipe its national identity off the face of the earth. Assyria, Babylonia, Egypt, Greece, Rome, the Ottoman Empire—all tried it at the peak of their power, and all failed. Italy was favored early as the most fertile ground for the development of the church, but it abused God's favor by forging a new type of political-ecclesiastical power structure which zealously kept the Bible out of the language and out of the hands of the common people. It was not long before Italy and the rest of Europe were plunged into the Dark Ages, when ignorance and superstition, for almost 1,000 years, replaced God's Word as a way of life.

France and Germany were offered the opportunity to light the fires of reformation. France forfeited its chance by yielding to Italy and allowing the massacre of approximately one million Bible-believing Christians—more popularly known as "heretics"—who had obtained and taught copies of the Scriptures translated into the tongue of Southern France. Under relentless state-church persecution, the movement was snuffed out, as far as France was concerned. The Protestant Reformation blazed forth in sixteenth-century Germany to bring an end to the millenium of darkness, but we have seen Germany since that time turn from the Bible to humanism. Germany has been a world battleground ever since.

Historians point out that the three great periods of England's past were under (1) Alfred the Great, who ordered that every subject in the kingdom be instructed in the Scriptures ahead of anything else; (2) Queen Elizabeth, who was the first to insist that the Bible be given a prominent role in coronation ceremonies; and (3) Queen Victoria, who said: "That book accounts for the supremacy of England." In the present generation, England is not demonstrating that historic love for God's Word that accompanied its times of greatness, and finds itself, as a nation, at one of its lowest ebbs morally, economically, and politically. Other factors are involved, of course, but I am convinced that the correlation is not a coincidence.

Russia has outlawed the Bible, and its people have lived in a "free" version of collectivized slavery ever since, behind an Iron Curtain they are not at liberty to lift or even to listen through. When the daughter of the late Premier Josef Stalin defected to this country and requested American citizenship, she gave as her basic motivation the discovery that she could not live "without God in the heart." A contemporary high official in the Communist Party has more recently admitted in a public statement that Communism is failing to meet the innermost needs of its people. Obviously, it was not conceived in the mind of a Bible-hating Karl Marx to achieve that end. The Bible, on the other hand, was prepared by the Holy Spirit of God for that express purpose.

The nation we live in was founded by men and women who brought their Bibles with them, and the United States Constitution was the first political document in history which could be said to derive directly from the Ten Commandments of the Old Testament and the Sermon on the Mount of the New Testament. The land has been blessed with freedom and prosperity and peace, above all other nations of the past two centuries. Holding on to the immutable truth of the Bible is the only insurance we have of the continuation of God's blessing upon us as a people. If the patterns of history mean anything, America can not minimize God's Word without following the course of all other nations which have forfeited interest in scriptural wisdom. In every case, their history was recorded in advance: "My people are destroyed for lack of knowledge"

(Hos. 4:6).

Let Go and Let God

If I need the Bible so desperately in my life, and if history indicates the Bible is an integral factor in national life, don't you need the Bible, too? If you ever have any of the kinds of problems listed below, look up the appropriate Scripture and read it out of context—not as coming from Daniel or James or Solomon or Joel—but as God's Word speaking directly to you today:

Afraid? Psalm 27:1,14

Can't understand disappointment? Romans 8:38-39

Bothered by the prosperity of the ungodly? Psalm 73:12-18

Tempted? 1 Corinthians 10:13

Doubting God's mercy? Psalm 103:8-18

Threatened with harm? Psalm 56:4,11

Tired? Isaiah 40:30-31

No friends? Proverbs 18:24

Worrying a lot? Philippians 4:5-7

Discouraged by recurring sin? Romans 7:19-23

Feel inferior? 1 Corinthians 15:10

Prayers not being answered? Isaiah 59:2

Questioning civic duty? Romans 13:7

Ashamed to tell it like it is? Proverbs 28:23

Can't overcome grief? Psalm 127:2

Finding it hard to live right? 1 Peter 4:14

Confused? Micah 6:8

Suffering physically? Psalm 41:3

Depressed? John 14:27

These are merely examples of myriad situations in which the Bible can talk to you if you let it. The list here is only a meager beginning, and there's no particular magic implied in the texts selected above. The point is that as you begin to lean on the Bible, to depend on it for daily guidance and restoration, and to believe its promises, you'll find that it has a great deal to say to you privately.

If doubts persist, it's time to recognize the roadblock: SELF. Most of us do what we want to do, concentrating on pleasing ourselves at any cost. God knows what we need, and for that reason he has placed his Word right in the center of our path, wanting us to place it in the center of our lives. Self-reliance is a virtue until it begins to outweigh concern for others and dependence upon the Creator; from there it quickly goes down the scale of selfishness. The root of selfishness is rebellion against God—sin, the Bible calls it—and the fruit of selfishness is inevitably doubt.

There is a little poem of defiance that has caught the fancy and admiration of several generations of young rebels seeking to establish the gospel of self-sufficiency. I was one of them, and for many years William Ernest Henley's familiar "Invictus" ("Unconquered") was my campaign song. Admiration for the author's heroic refusal to collapse under extremely trying personal testing was replaced by my own brand of arrogance, which his words seemed to express for me. But now that I can proclaim with thanksgiving that my rebellious soul has been conquered by the love of a forgiving Christ revealed in the Bible, I would rewrite those lines and give them a new title:

Invictus	Victus

Out of the night that covers me,
  Black as the Pit from pole to pole,
I thank whatever gods may be
  For my unconquerable soul.
	Out of the light that covers me,
	  Bright as the sun from pole to pole,
	I thank the God I know to be
	  For my regenerated soul.

In the fell clutch of circumstance
  I have not winced nor cried aloud.
Under the bludgeonings of chance
  My head is bloody, but unbowed.
	In the fell clutch of sin's embrace
	  I winced and cried to Him aloud.
	Under the blood of redeeming grace
	  My head is crowned, and humbly bowed.

Beyond this place of wrath and tears
  Looms but the Horror of the shade,
And yet the menace of the years
  Finds, and shall find me, unafraid.
	Beyond this place of joy and tears
	  Lie Heaven's glories He has made,
	And thus the menace of the years
	  Finds, and shall find me, unafraid.

It matters not how strait the gate
  How charged with punishments
    the scroll,
I am the master of my fate:
  I am the captain of my soul.
	It matters all how strait the gate
	  How cleared of punishments
	    the scroll,
	For God is master of my fate:
	  And Christ is the Captain of my soul.

The key to victory, paradoxically, is surrender. The braggadocio of a hopeless, hapless, hardened will may sound heroic, but it is the saddest of human tragedies.